"Our basic book is the Bible. But anyone in ministry will be further enriched by getting acquainted with the pastoral classics discussed in this book. (A classic is a distinguished book that speaks to every generation and doesn't have to be rewritten.) Whether you are new to ministry or a veteran, the books discussed in this guide can help you better understand yourself and your calling beyond what you may have learned from textbooks and lectures. These classics offer enlightenment as well as entertainment, and this book is one of the best guides I have seen. I highly recommend it."

—**Warren W. Wiersbe**, author; former pastor, Moody Church

"Many pastors know the power of a well-chosen citation from Kierkegaard or Dostoevsky when preaching to others. But for pastors who are tired, discouraged, isolated, trapped in some lethal sin, or in danger of losing their faith, here is an ideal guide to find in the classics the deepest, most relevant, emotionally gripping wisdom to preach to oneself. May God use it to revive many of us, remind us of the height from which we have fallen, and restore us to our first love."

—**Gordon P. Hugenberger**, senior minister, Park Street Church, Boston

"*Pastors in the Classics* is a splendid and unique guide to the portraits of pastoral ministry found in the great works of Western literature. The useful information provided here will be enlightening, and the insightful commentary appreciated by anyone who has ever pastored a flock. Lovers of great literature will find their reading more enjoyable and their understanding deepened by this satisfying work."

—**Devin Brown**, department of English, Asbury University; author of *Inside Narnia*

"We come to know ourselves—and others—through stories. Here the authors invite us into literary worlds replete with stories of pastors: pastors who preach and suffer, who sin and repent, who fail in small and spectacular ways, who stand always in need of grace. If we accept the invitation to enter these tales, we will emerge challenged and encouraged, our hearts returned to love of God and neighbor."

—**Susan Felch**, professor of English, Calvin College

PASTORS *in* THE CLASSICS

PASTORS *in* THE CLASSICS

Timeless Lessons *on* Life and Ministry *from* World Literature

LELAND RYKEN, PHILIP RYKEN, AND TODD WILSON

BakerBooks

a division of Baker Publishing Group
Grand Rapids, Michigan

Published by Baker Books
a division of Baker Publishing Group
P.O. Box 6287, Grand Rapids, MI 49516-6287
www.bakerbooks.com

Printed in the United States of America

Library of Congress Cataloging-in-Publication Data
Ryken, Leland.
   Pastors in the classics : timeless lessons on life and ministry from world
literature / Leland Ryken, Philip Ryken, and Todd Wilson.
       p.   cm.
   ISBN 978-0-8010-7197-3 (pbk.)
   1. Clergy in literature. I. Ryken, Philip Graham, 1966– II. Wilson, Todd A.,
1976– III. Title.
PN56.5.C5R95 2012
809′.9338253—dc23   2011032005

12   13   14   15   16   17   18   7   6   5   4   3   2   1

Contents

Introduction

This book was conceived when the two authors who are pastors independently envisioned a book that explores the image of the pastor and issues of ministry in literary masterpieces. Both would-be authors also independently requested the literary scholar on the authorial team to serve as coauthor. The convergence of these ingredients was sufficient to launch the project.

What Kind of Book Is This?

This book is a road map to literary masterpieces in which the pastor's experience is a major part of the story. In fact, this book contains nearly everything that a reader or discussion leader needs in order to get started on an exploration of the pastor in literature.

The first part of the book is a reader's guide to twelve important literary classics in which pastors are the mainspring of the action. These masterworks were written in four centuries and cover seven nationalities. The analyses of these works go beyond description to interpretation. Furthermore, each chapter highlights a specific feature of pastoral ministry that the literary work itself puts before us. Reflection/discussion questions are part of these chapters.

The second part of the book is a handbook—a reference book that defines the canon of literary masterpieces that deal with the pastor's experience. The entries in this section give all the information a reader needs when selecting literary works that deal with pastors.

In summary, this book is both a reader's guide to major works and a reference book containing information about the field as a whole.

Aims and Goals of This Book

The first goal of this book is to facilitate the reading of some great works of literature. We hope the works covered in this book will emerge in readers' imaginations as literary delights. They are works of literature first of all and works providing insight into the pastor's life within that parameter. It is important to note additionally that the works surveyed are not narrowly concerned with issues of ministry but actually cover all of life. For example, T. S. Eliot's play *Murder in the Cathedral* portrays not only the final days in the life of a saint but also the life of the common citizens of Canterbury in their daily routine of hopes and fears.

Literature has a unique ability to speak to the whole person, and the books surveyed in this volume can teach and move readers in a way that nonliterary books about ministry do not. This is partly a difference between "showing" and "telling." A contemporary book on issues in ministry might *tell* a minister not to enter into sexual relations with a woman in the congregation, while Nathaniel Hawthorne's famous story *shows* why a minister should not do so.

Second, we chose works in which the pastor's life is a major ingredient. Accordingly, the commentary focuses chiefly on the ways in which the works portray and clarify issues in the minister's life and vocation. The table of contents of this book shows at a glance the issues the respective literary works address—scandalous clergy, hidden sin in a preacher's life, the dilemma of the unworthiness of ministers to do God's work, and so forth. The books chosen for this volume can help to shape the spiritual life of people in ministry.

Third, most of the works covered in this book place the minister's life within a broader Christian context. The works thus incline toward the broad category known as Christian literature—literature that portrays experiences that are important to Christians and that endorses Christian doctrines. For most of the works, therefore, the usual rewards of reading Christian literature will be present, including reflection on the Christian life, affirmation of a Christian worldview, and nurture of the soul. John Milton said that one of the effects of reading Christian literature is that it "sets the affections [the old word for emotions] in right tune." The works discussed in this book generally make the grade and can legitimately be called devotional reading. Thus, *The Scarlet Letter* is a Christian classic in its portrayal of salvation, quite apart from the fact that it deals with ministerial issues.

How Should This Book Be Used?

This book is first of all an aid to an individual reader's mastery of the literary works included in the book. This book shares the goal of all literary criticism, namely, the enhancement of a reader's enjoyment and understanding of the works that are discussed.

Second, we have had a continuous eye on how to foster group discussion of the chosen works. Such discussion could occur equally well in an academic course, a seminar, or a book discussion group. In the sections bearing the heading "For Reflection or Discussion," the questions are intended as prompts either to individual reflection or group discussion. Ministers and Christian leaders might find it useful to have their own small group discussions and even form accountability groups.

Third, readers who are themselves pastors or Christian leaders should read the literary works surveyed in this book as potentially revealing important things about themselves and their vocation. One outcome might be an improved ability to make right moral choices. Another is insight into the Christian leader's spiritual formation. Choosing good priorities in ministry is a plausible outcome for some of the works surveyed. Vicariously living the experiences of Chaucer's religious professionals, or the local preacher in Puritan Boston, or the whiskey priest in Mexico, or the Archbishop of Canterbury martyred for his faith should help religious leaders "get it right" in their own lives.

Finally, this book is a readers' guide to the works that we cover. It is not a substitute for reading the works but instead presupposes that they have been read. We have therefore included publication information about the works that we discuss to make it easy to locate them.

How to Read a Literary Book

A work of literature needs to be read and analyzed in a manner that accords with the nature of literature. A literary work differs from ordinary expository or informational writing at the levels of both form and content. A useful framework for understanding literature is to think in terms of the literary author's task being threefold.

The literary author's first task is to present human experience. This means that the subject of literature is human experience concretely presented. A work of literature is not primarily a delivery system for an idea; it is an embodiment of human experience. A work of literature is a house in which we are invited to take up residence and out of which we look at life. The lesson a reader needs to learn from this is not to try immediately to reduce a literary work to a set of ideas. A reader's first task is to relive the work as completely as possible. *The Scarlet Letter* can never be reduced to an idea, such as the need for a minister not to lead a hidden life of sin and hypocrisy; instead, we need to relive Dimmesdale's experience of that principle.

Another way to grasp this dimension of literature is to acknowledge that authors create an imagined world that we enter as we read. As readers we need to become citizens of this imagined world, noting its properties as fully as possible. T. S. Eliot's *Murder in the Cathedral* is refreshing partly because it is an instance of a modern writer who actually believes in the reality of heaven and hell. The imagined world of a literary work, moreover, is understood to be the author's picture of reality—of how things truly are in our own world.

As we inhabit the author's world, we first of all look *at* it but eventually also *out of* it to our own experiences. Elmer Gantry is not only a character in a book but also a person we continually meet in real life (and possibly when we look in the mirror).

Second, in addition to *presenting* human experience for our contemplation, an author *interprets* the experiences he or she portrays. A novelist once said that in order to compose a story authors must have some picture of the world *and of what is right and wrong in that world.* In other words, authors impose an interpretive grid on their material. They select and mold their material in such a way as to exhibit their worldview and moral vision. For example, Hawthorne leaves us in no doubt about the need to confess sin instead of escaping from it, as well as the possibility of God's forgiveness.

The literary author's third task is to present literary form, technique, and beauty for a reader's enjoyment and artistic enrichment. Literature is an art form as well as a comment about life. Although this book focuses on the pastor's life and issues in ministry, it would be an impoverishment to focus so single-mindedly on the religious content that the artistic rewards of literary form are slighted. It is our hope that no reader of this book will feel it to be inappropriate to revel in the artistic dimension of the works as self-rewarding and as worthy of attention in its own right and quite apart from the comments that a work makes about the pastor's life. Whatever a writer chooses to put into a work is worthy of our attention and delight. All the authors discussed in this book were masters of storytelling, character portrayal, description, and words.

Portraits of Ministers

A final word can be said about how to assemble a character portrait from a work of literature. While it is possible to explore the twelve major works covered in this book without formally compiling a portrait of the pastor (and for some works multiple pastors), nonetheless a complete analysis of these works would benefit from such an exercise. Below are four questions that will be useful in assembling a "portrait of the minister":

1. What roles does the pastor fill in this book? Examples might include preacher, counselor, spiritual leader, community member, friend, spouse, parent.
2. What relationships are important for the pastor in this book?
3. What are the pastor's personal character traits in this book?
4. What is the pastor's place in the social context portrayed in the book? Is his sphere limited to the church, or does it move beyond that to the family and/or community?

PART 1

A Guide to Masterworks
of Clerical Literature

1

The Canterbury Tales

Scandalous Clergy

Should not shepherds feed the sheep? You eat the fat, you clothe yourselves with the wool, you slaughter the fat ones, but you do not feed the sheep.

Ezekiel 34:2–3

Geoffrey Chaucer is one of the most famous portrayers of professional clergymen. Yet his best-known work is an anomaly in this book on pastors in the literary classics, inasmuch as Chaucer's masterpiece is neither a novel nor a play. As a result, we need to ferret out his portraits of clerics in a series of individual rooms of a mansion called *The Canterbury Tales*.

Chaucer's famous work is an anthology of separate stories comprising all the most popular narrative genres of the later Middle Ages, such as romance, mock epic, tragedy, fable, and saint's legend. To bring these self-contained stories together in a single work, Chaucer hit upon the idea of a group of pilgrims traveling from London to Canterbury. Within that enterprise, his main strategy was a stroke of genius: he parceled out his favorite individual stories to pilgrims who could plausibly be the tellers of particular stories.

Of course, Chaucer needed a way to introduce the pilgrimage and the cast of characters. The resulting literary segment is known as "The General Prologue" to *The Canterbury Tales*. It consists of an introduction to the pilgrimage itself and individual portraits of most of the pilgrims. The richest portrait is of Chaucer the narrator, but we need to assemble his portrait indirectly.

Our approach for this chapter is first to look at the portraits that are most relevant to our focus in this book. After that, we will explore a self-revealing story told by one of the clerics on the pilgrimage.

The individual portraits in "The General Prologue" belong to a genre that we know as the character sketch but that in premodern times people simply

17

Author: Geoffrey Chaucer (ca. 1343–1400)

Nationality: English

Date of composition: 1387–1400

Available editions: Originally written in Middle English. Modern English translations are plentiful, but best of all are dual-language editions that print the Middle English version on the left page and a modern translation on the facing right page; Bantam and Barnes & Noble have dual-language editions.

Genres: poetic narrative, pilgrimage story, character sketch, satire

Setting for the story: the road from London to Canterbury, late 1300s

Main characters: Chaucer the narrator (a pilgrim on the trip who narrates what the other pilgrims are like and the stories they told); two dozen other pilgrims who come alive in our imaginations when the focus shifts individually to them

Plot summary: Some thirty pilgrims (including Chaucer the narrator, a fictional alter ego to Chaucer the author) assemble at the Tabard Inn in the London suburb of Southwark, ready to embark on a religious pilgrimage to Canterbury to visit the shrine of Thomas à Becket (whose martyrdom forms the story material for T. S. Eliot's play *Murder in the Cathedral*). Their host at the inn is so captivated by the group that he decides to join them, and he further proposes that to while away the time the pilgrims tell stories as they travel on horseback to Canterbury and back. "The General Prologue" to the collection of stories provides the narrative framework for the pilgrimage and also brief sketches of most of the pilgrims. The rest of *The Canterbury Tales* consists of an anthology of medieval narrative genres, with interspersed narrative links that bring us back to the story of the progress of the traveling group on its trip.

---

called "the character." Chaucer is unsurpassed in his ability to make a whole person come alive with just a few deftly chosen details. He was adept at visualizing a character and capturing the root trait of a character, often clinching the matter with a quick glimpse into the inner person. Most of the portraits have a satiric edge to them, meaning they expose human vice or folly. Finally, people in the Middle Ages loved allegory and symbolism. As a result, some of the details in the portraits are a virtual code language that we, more than six centuries later, need help deciphering.

The Ideal Minister: The Portrait of the Parson

Of the portraits that make up "The General Prologue," only one or two are wholly idealized or favorable. The parson belongs to this elite group. His portrait is found in lines 465–516. While most of the portraits in "The General

Prologue" require that we approach them with a hermeneutic of suspicion—looking for negative features under a sometimes glowing exterior—with the portrait of the parson we need to lay our suspicions aside. Our working premise should be that Chaucer is offering us a model to admire and emulate, as well as a foil that sets off the failings of all the other clerics on the pilgrimage.

Probably the best way to assimilate Chaucer's model pastor is to work our way through the portrait line by line. Almost everything is stated directly, in keeping with the parson's humble and down-to-earth way of exercising his calling. To lend structure to the analysis, we should be aware that Chaucer mingles four ingredients in his portrait of an ideal pastor: the pastoral duties that belong to the parson's calling, how the parson views himself, the parson's attitude toward his flock, and the parson's character qualities and spiritual virtues.

FOR REFLECTION OR DISCUSSION

Why would you love to have this parson as your minister? In what ways does Chaucer's parson serve as a corrective to tendencies that are sometimes found in clergymen? What forces on the contemporary scene might make it difficult to attain the ideal that Chaucer puts before us in the portrait of his parson?

Self-Indulgence: The Portrait of the Monk

Chaucer's parson stands as a foil to all the other clerical portraits he composed. Starting with the portrait of the monk (lines 165–207 in "The General Prologue"), we need to read with a hermeneutic of suspicion. In doing so, it is helpful to know an important fact about Chaucer the narrator (as distinct from Chaucer the author). Chaucer created a fictional persona for himself when he included himself as one of the pilgrims. This persona, whom literary critics simply call Chaucer the narrator, is an obtuse and unreliable narrator. His *descriptions* of the pilgrims are of course all that we have and are presumably accurate, but his *evaluations* of them are often unreliable. In particular, Chaucer the narrator is much impressed by signs of external success, and he tends to take various clerical figures on their own terms, not realizing the degree to which this often condemns them *as clerics*. Of course, this tendency to admire clergy according to worldly standards of success is perennial.

An example of the narrator's unreliable judgment occurs in the opening line of the monk's portrait, where the narrator tells us that the monk was a "splendid" or "superlatively fine" monk. In fact, he is the opposite. To see the full extent of this, we need to know a bit of context from beyond the poem itself. Monks were supposed to renounce worldly pleasures, and they were commanded to remain cloistered within the physical confines of the

19

monastery. They were expected to spend their time studying, working, and worshiping. Finally, monks took vows of poverty, chastity, and obedience to the monastic rules.

When measured by these monastic ideals, almost every detail in the portrait constitutes a violation of the ideal. In particular, we should work our way through the portrait looking for evidence of the following: an obsession with recreational activities (especially hunting), living an affluent lifestyle, love of luxurious clothing, overeating and indulging a gourmet appetite, and laziness in studying and working.

FOR REFLECTION OR DISCUSSION

How often, and in what ways, have you observed the tendencies portrayed in Chaucer's monk in real-life ministers? What examples from your life stand out as a contrast to such abuses? To what degree might we see in the monk the perversion of things that are good and legitimate in principle and within bounds?

Sex and Gluttony: The Portrait of the Friar

With the portrait of the friar (lines 208–71 of "The General Prologue"), Chaucer pushes his indictment of the clergy in a sexual direction. He sounds the keynote in the first line of the portrait when he calls the friar "wanton and merry." We then read many variations on the theme of the friar's dalliance with the young women and wives in the territory in which he plies his trade as a professional beggar (actually a lucrative profession for the friar). Some of the details need deciphering: the friar's white neck (line 337) was, according to medieval symbolism, a sign of lechery; his peddler's wares (lines 233–34) were aids to seducing married women; his songs and fiddle playing (lines 235–37) were likewise helps in the friar's sexual exploits.

A second unifying thread in the portrait of the monk is his skill at making money. He even uses his clerical calling to get rich. For example, he had the power of hearing people's confession of sin, and he made it a practice to charge a monetary penalty (which he pocketed) as penance (lines 218–32). Instead of seeking the company of the down-and-outers of his society, he kept company with the wealthy. He is portly through his love of extravagant eating (indicating that he has the money to eat at expensive inns).

FOR REFLECTION OR DISCUSSION

We should begin by conducting a close reading of the text: what details add to the cumulative portrait of sexual dalliance, obsession with wealth, and an indulgent life in regard to eating and drinking? Then we can reflect on contemporary manifestations of these abuses. Why have sexual sins afflicted the clerical profession? How do ministers sometimes slip into a luxurious lifestyle? This is also as good a place as any to tackle a question that is appropriate to Chaucer and to many (most?) literary authors who have portrayed ministers: what do you make of the fact that the tendency has been strong to portray pastors in a negative light? Numerous answers are possible, so we should not settle for an easy disposition of the question.

The Devil Calling Sinners to Repentance: The Pardoner and His Tale

Medieval "pardoners" were clerics who engaged in as many as three activities—selling indulgences, selling relics, and preaching. The money that pardoners raised through these activities was theoretically used for church activities, but the opportunity for pardoners to pocket the money they raised was inherent in their vocation.

The portrait of the pardoner (lines 671–716 in "The General Prologue") repeats the same emphases that are present in the portrait of the friar, so the commentary above can be applied here as well. There are some important differences, however. The pardoner is not a lady's man who charms women but an effeminate homosexual. Instead of peddling knives and pins to housewives, the pardoner has a bag full of fraudulent relics that he sells to gullible commoners. The institutional key to the pardoner's moneymaking success is not confession and penance but preaching accompanied by appeals for financial donations to religious causes.

The story the pardoner tells is an extension of what we learn about him in "The General Prologue." It is customary for commentators to speak of the pardoner's "prologue and tale" for the following reasons: Chaucer chose to allot three hundred lines in which the pardoner leads up to his story (which turns out to be an "example story" within a model sermon). In these three hundred lines, the pardoner describes to his fellow pilgrims how he goes about a typical preaching assignment. The opening line introduces this situation: "'My lords,' said he, 'when I preach in church . . .'" What follows is a how-to lesson in homiletics. The prologue also belongs to the genre known as the confession, inasmuch as the pardoner is totally uninhibited in admitting his greed and deceitfulness. In yet another twist, his confession is actually a form of bragging.

For our purposes, the prologue to the pardoner's eventual story is the relevant text. A good avenue to analysis is to divide the material into separate strands. One interspersed ingredient is the account the pardoner gives of his pulpit style. He is highly oratorical. He is an arm-waver and head-bobber. He denounces sins of the flesh in melodramatic fashion.

21

A second ingredient is the information the pardoner gives about his favorite sermon content. The theme of every sermon is that the love of money is the root of all evil. The pardoner laces his sermons with stories that "ignorant people love" to hear. He speaks "a few words in Latin" to "give color and flavor" to his preaching.

Third, the pardoner shares in boasting fashion the techniques by which he induces his audiences to contribute money. He displays containers full of fraudulent relics that he coerces his listeners to buy. His power play in this regard is to announce that if members of the audience have committed a sin so terrible that they do not dare confess it, they should not come forward, but if they are exempt from such sins, they should show it by coming forward to buy relics. And of course his sermon topic of the evil of money has the effect of inclining people to part with their money.

Fourth, intermingled with the foregoing ingredients are confessional statements by the pardoner about his hypocrisy and greed. For example, he is forthright that in preaching against the sin of avarice he is preaching against the very vice he practices. He is open about how his homiletic practices are designed to impress the ignorant. He calls his selling of fraudulent relics a trick. He speaks of the "falsehoods" that he tells. He even says he preaches "for no cause but covetousness."

Finally, the pardoner forces his fellow pilgrims (and us as readers) to come to grips with the issue that Graham Greene expanded to novel length in his book *The Power and the Glory*, namely, the question of whether a flawed minister can nonetheless produce the right spiritual effect in his congregants. The pardoner's viewpoint is that although he himself "is guilty of the sin" of avarice, nonetheless, he "can make other folk repent" of that very sin, with the implication that the latter fact is all that matters.

FOR REFLECTION OR DISCUSSION

Our first task is to get to know Chaucer's pardoner as fully as possible. What things make up the satiric portrait of this scandalous clergyman? What clerical vices are obvious to anyone who sees the pardoner? What hidden recesses make the portrait even more revolting? Then we can reflect on real-life acquaintance with the type. Where in your own experience have you encountered a minister like Chaucer's pardoner? How does the pastoral calling make some of these abuses possible? Finally, we need to come to our own conclusion about the central question posed by the pardoner's confession: since no minister is perfect, obviously ministerial flaws to some degree do not inhibit the spiritual effectiveness of a minister. Equally obvious, a minister's behavior does matter to us. Where do you draw the line?

2

The Scarlet Letter

Hidden Sin and Its Consequences

For when I kept silent, my bones wasted away
> through my groaning all day long.
For day and night your hand was heavy upon me;
> my strength was dried up as by the heat of summer.
I acknowledged my sin to you,
> and I did not cover my iniquity;
I said, "I will confess my transgressions to the LORD,"
> and you forgave the iniquity of my sin.

Psalm 32:3–5

The Scarlet Letter might well be *the* American classic. From the time of its appearance, it has been a cultural icon. Even people who haven't read it know *about* it, and therein lies a problem: there is perhaps no work of literature that has occasioned as many misconceptions as this one.

For the record, therefore, here are four things that are *not* true about *The Scarlet Letter*. (1) In the prologue to the story, the narrator, picturing himself as a customs officer in Salem, describes coming upon an embroidered scarlet letter *A*. This is a purely fictitious claim; Hawthorne never discovered such a letter in the Salem Custom House. (2) There is no historical evidence that in Puritan New England adulterers were forced to wear a scarlet letter *A* on their breasts. (3) The picture that Hawthorne paints of the Puritans is a satiric exaggeration, not an accurate account of the Puritans as they were in principle. Furthermore, although Hawthorne condemns Puritan *behavior* in his story, he affirms Puritan/Christian *doctrine* in the conclusion of his story. (4) Although the sin of adultery lies *behind* the action of the story, this is not

23

Author: Nathaniel Hawthorne (1804–64)

Nationality: American

Date of first publication: 1850

Approximate number of pages: 250

Available editions: Bantam, Dover Thrift, Norton, Penguin, Random House, etc.

Genres: romantic novel (with the adjective *romantic* meaning that elements of the supernatural or marvelous are mingled with the prevailing realism of the story), historical fiction

Setting for the story: Boston in Puritan times (mid-seventeenth century)

Main characters: Arthur Dimmesdale, the Puritan minister of the town; Hester Prynne, a married woman with whom Dimmesdale produced an illegitimate daughter named Pearl; Roger Chillingworth, the husband of Hester who arrives belatedly in the town and seeks to destroy Dimmesdale as an act of revenge; the Puritan community as a group. No one of these dominates the story more than the others, but inasmuch as Dimmesdale's salvation on the scaffold resolves the action, by the story's end he has emerged as the protagonist.

Plot summary: The story opens with the exposure of Hester Prynne on a scaffold, holding an infant daughter whose father she refuses to disclose. In punishment, she is ostracized by the Puritan community and forced to wear a scarlet letter *A* on her bosom. The father of the girl is the town minister, Arthur Dimmesdale, who is too weak-willed to shoulder his share of responsibility in the sin of adultery. Eventually, Hester's husband, Roger Chillingworth, arrives in Boston and takes up residence with Dimmesdale. He inflames Dimmesdale's sense of guilt, and the minister goes into a long physical and mental decline. In the climax of the story, Dimmesdale, on the verge of death, mounts the scaffold and confesses his sin, experiencing God's forgiveness as he does so.

a story about adultery or sex; it is about sin, guilt, hypocrisy (in the form of hidden sin), confession of sin, and forgiveness.

A final preliminary that needs to be asserted is that our focus on the minister in the story is in keeping with the contours Hawthorne himself laid down. It is true that the book gives equal attention to Hester and Dimmesdale. Hester represents the worldview of nineteenth-century Romanticism, which elevated feeling to the highest value and despised civilized institutions. Dimmesdale embodies the Christian worldview. Hawthorne lets these two fight it out for supremacy, and one of the most important things to note, quite apart from this book's emphasis on the minister's calling, is the ways in which the romantic and Christian worldviews are evident in the attitudes expressed by Hester and Dimmesdale, respectively. But it is crucial to note that in the climactic scaffold scene, the story itself demonstrates the triumph of Christian grace and forgiveness over romantic feeling. Dimmesdale's attainment of salvation, and not Hester's impulse to leave town, resolves the action.

The main ministerial themes highlighted in the discussion that follows are in evidence throughout the story, instead of being introduced in sequence as the story unfolds. Each of our chosen themes will emerge most clearly if readers follow them individually through the story in multiple readings.

How *Not* to Relate to a Female Parishioner

Hawthorne titled his seventeenth chapter "The Pastor and His Parishioner." It is difficult to imagine a more ironic title than this. It names the external relationship between Dimmesdale and Hester, but it conceals the real nature of their relationship, which has been intimate and sexual.

The story does not give us a detailed account of sexual sin (which took place before the action of the story begins), but it nonetheless raises the issue of a minister's dealings with a female congregant. Although the story does not ask us to dwell on the dynamics and details of the sexual relationship between Dimmesdale and Hester, there is hardly a page of the book on which we are not aware of sexual sin, chiefly because of the presence of the offspring of the adultery.

The story contains hints of how "the pastor and his parishioner" managed to stray into their forbidden relationship. In the background lies Hester's ill-advised marriage to Roger Chillingworth. Chillingworth, in turn, had failed to show up in Boston as planned, leaving the attractive Hester alone. We infer some type of romantic relationship between the abandoned Hester and the bachelor pastor. Mainly, though, the story focuses on the life of suffering that the illicit relationship produced. When it comes to cautioning a preacher not to take the forbidden step, it is hard to beat *The Scarlet Letter* for sounding the warning.

FOR REFLECTION OR DISCUSSION

From one point of view, the entire story is an exploration of the bad effects of a minister's mismanaging his relationship with a female church member; exactly what are those effects? As Rev. Dimmesdale disintegrates as a result of his guilty conscience, he becomes such a weak figure that the dynamic parishioner Hester actually counsels her pastor; within the logic of the story, how does her advice constitute bad counsel? If the story shows us how not to relate to someone of the opposite sex, what conclusions can we reach about how to relate?

The Minister as Sinner

The unifying action of *The Scarlet Letter* is Dimmesdale's career as a sinner. The story itself is an anatomy of how sin works in a minister's life, including the manifold nature of that sin and (more importantly) its effect in the minister's life.

Until the very end of the story (chap. 23), the narrative is an ever-expanding picture of Dimmesdale's sins. The picture begins in the second chapter when Hester resists the pressure to reveal the identity of her infant daughter's father. Dimmesdale himself is too weak-willed and fearful of losing his standing in the community to confess his sexual sin. The initial sins of adultery and cover-up are what set the entire steamroller of evil into motion. In keeping with Hawthorne's strategy of setting the romantic and Christian worldviews in competition, throughout the first half of the story Hester is a sympathetic foil (contrast) to the minister's weakness.

As bad as the sins of sexual indulgence, moral cowardice, and abandonment of a persecuted woman are, as the story unfolds, hypocrisy emerges as Rev. Dimmesdale's most intensely felt sin. As the preacher makes veiled hints of his sexual sin in his sermons, his parishioners idealize him even more for what seems to be extreme piety. In a summary statement, we read, "It is inconceivable, the agony with which this public veneration tortured him" (chap. 6). The contrast between Hester and Dimmesdale is primarily the contrast between confessed sin and concealed sin, and the mainspring of the book is the fact and effects of hidden sin in a minister who appears to be an exemplary Christian.

FOR REFLECTION OR DISCUSSION

There can be little doubt that Hawthorne had a particular knack for portraying the effects of sin in an individual's life. In turn, one of the best ways to get to know Arthur Dimmesdale as fully as possible is to trace the litany of sins and failures he displays as the story unfolds; what are those sins and failures? Of course, literary characters are representative of people more generally, so we can legitimately view the sins of Dimmesdale as failings that ministers are prone to confront. Exactly how did Dimmesdale come to commit the sins that he did, and what insights into the minister's life does this analysis yield?

The Minister's Guilty Conscience

It is a truism that in *The Scarlet Letter* Hawthorne gave American literature its greatest portrayal of guilt, just as Shakespeare did for English literature in his play *Macbeth*. The dynamics of guilt operate on two levels in Hawthorne's story.

One level is the psychological. As we accompany Dimmesdale on his experiment in concealed sin, we see more and more ways in which his psyche and emotional self progressively deteriorate as a result of his guilty conscience. Hawthorne tells this story of the psychology of guilt in multiple ways. One is through habitual actions that Dimmesdale adopts as part of his futile attempt to cope with his guilt—actions like placing his hand over his heart, for example, or scourging himself physically in private. Another motif that is pursued systematically is what today we call psychosomatic symptoms—what the demonic Chillingworth calls "a strange sympathy betwixt soul and body" (chap. 10). A third technique at which Hawthorne was adept is the narration of what is going on inside Dimmesdale's thinking, a technique that literary critics call psychological realism.

Of course, it is difficult to disentangle what is psychological and what is spiritual in the losing battle Dimmesdale fights with his inner guilt. Probably Hawthorne did not intend that we differentiate the two. Dimmesdale's futile visit to the scaffold under the cloak of night (chap. 12), for example, fits the psychological motif of the impulse to return to the scene of a crime, but it also enacts the spiritual compulsion of the guilty sinner to find forgiveness through confession. Depending on a reader's own theology of sin, the progressive decline of Dimmesdale is a spiritual collapse, perhaps modeled on David's statement about unrelieved guilt in Psalm 32:3: "When I kept silent, my bones wasted away through my groaning all day long." But the story is based equally on Psalm 32:5: "I acknowledged my sin to you [God], . . . and you forgave the iniquity of my sin." Dimmesdale finds relief in confession to God and forgiveness from him in the climactic confession scene (chap. 23), where the unfolding action is couched in specifically spiritual and theological language.

FOR REFLECTION OR DISCUSSION

Hawthorne is such a genius at portraying the psychology of guilt that it would be easy to overlook the spiritual analysis the story also provides. What hints can you find in the story that Hawthorne is telling a story of spiritual guilt and forgiveness on both psychological and spiritual levels? What theology of sin and forgiveness does the story express?

When a Minister Opens Himself to Bad Counsel and Influence

Not least of Dimmesdale's problems is the influence and advice he receives from those around him. Two of these bad influences are blatant, while the third is subtle.

First there is the Puritan community. Hawthorne treats Puritan *behavior* satirically (in contrast to Puritan *theology*, which he portrays as a sympathetic norm at the end of the book). Satire is the exposure of an abuse, and satirists typically exaggerate their real-life materials. Puritan behavior in the story is rigid and unforgiving of offense, and its influence on Dimmesdale is primarily to drive him underground and lead him to repress his sin and guilt. There is even a hint at one point that Dimmesdale feared death as a penalty if he acknowledged his adultery (chap. 17).

Roger Chillingworth, Hester's husband who lives with Dimmesdale and ostensibly serves as his doctor, rather quickly comes to the conclusion that Dimmesdale was the sexual partner of his wife. Thereupon Chillingworth systematically fans the flames of Dimmesdale's guilty conscience. In the climactic confession scene, as Dimmesdale receives God's forgiveness, Chillingworth repeatedly mutters, "Thou hast escaped me." In the last chapter of the book, we learn that once Chillingworth's opportunity for revenge was taken from him, he died within a year, deprived of his reason for living.

The subtle evil influence in the minister's life is Hester. In the middle of the book, when Hester and Dimmesdale meet in the forest, Hester proposes that she and Dimmesdale run away from the village that torments them. This is the enthronement of romantic impulse, choosing escape from society rather than confession of sin to God. For all her affectionate loyalty to Dimmesdale, Hester's proposal represents a temptation to abandon moral duty and God. The narrator editorializes this angle when he asserts, "Tempted by a dream of happiness," Dimmesdale "had yielded himself with deliberate choice . . . to what he knew was deadly sin. And the infectious poison of that sin had been thus rapidly diffused throughout his moral system" (chap. 20). On the verge of receiving God's forgiveness, Dimmesdale asks Hester, "Is not this better than what we dreamed of in the forest?" (chap. 23). And Hester, romantic spokesperson to the last, replies, "I know not."

For Reflection or Discussion

The first step is to see how the story itself embodies three types of detrimental influence: (1) succumbing to bad influences from a congregation in an effort to preserve oneself and one's standing in the Christian community; (2) unwittingly being manipulated by vengeful or simply destructive people; and (3) consciously abandoning duty and obligations to God because a sympathetic and winsome companion has offered escape as an appealing way out of a difficult situation. Where do you find evidence of each of these in the story? What forms do these pressures take in a minister's life (or any Christian's life) today?

The Minister as Penitent

The Scarlet Letter makes its points chiefly by the literary principle of negative example. This is to say that the book is a case study in how *not* to behave as a minister. As the foregoing discussion has implied, Rev. Dimmesdale is a walking bundle of ministerial pathologies. He derailed his entire life through a sexual fling with a young, married parishioner. He was too weak-willed to confess his sin. The more he concealed his sin, the more he collapsed into physical and mental ruin. To top it all off, the minister agreed to run away from his town and church with his female parishioner. It is all as up-to-date as the latest ministerial scandal.

But the greatest glory of Hawthorne's story is the surprise ending. After building up Hester as the sympathetic and engaging central figure in the first half of the book, Hawthorne then sets into motion a progressive moral dereliction in which Hester declines from the moral standard she had earlier exhibited to our admiration. Her dereliction is seen mainly in her enticement of Dimmesdale to run away with her instead of assuming moral and spiritual responsibility for his sin by confessing it and seeking God's forgiveness.

In the magnificent confession scene on the scaffold (chap. 23), Hawthorne tips his hand in favor of the Christian worldview and its belief that God's forgiveness of the sinner is the one thing needful. Step-by-step, Hawthorne places Dimmesdale on display as the ideal penitent. No book surveyed in this reader's guide gives better news to ministers than the conclusion of *The Scarlet Letter*, and *that* from an author who is not commonly regarded as a Christian writer. The good news that emerges at the end of *The Scarlet Letter* is that ministers can receive God's grace and forgiveness too, if they confess their sin.

The confession scene at the end of Hawthorne's classic story works out in leisurely narrative detail the command of James 5:16: "Confess your sins to one another . . . that you may be healed." Someone has correctly observed that Dimmesdale's spiritual and physical decline throughout most of the story runs parallel to his confusion about the nature of God. In the forest meeting with Hester, we read that "the conscience-stricken priest" said to Hester, "The judgment of God is on me. It is too mighty for me to struggle with" (chap. 17). In the climactic chapter of the book, Dimmesdale experiences God as a God of mercy rather than unrelenting judgment.

The sequence that any careful reader can trace in chapter 23 is as follows: (1) the minister's complete confession to the crowd of spectators (in contrast to an ineffectual nighttime "vigil" on the platform in chap. 7); (2) Dimmesdale's awareness that God is the one who has given him the strength to make his confession; (3) elaborate emphasis on God's mercy; (4) equal emphasis on the fact that Dimmesdale is making his confession of sin to God the divine judge as well as to his parishioners; and (5) human reconciliation (seen especially in Dimmesdale's relationship to his daughter Pearl) as an accompaniment to God's forgiveness. A literary critic has correctly said that *The Scarlet Letter* "is a complete vision of salvation."

It is important not to be deterred from seeing the triumph of grace in this story simply because generations of secular scholars have ignored its Christian ending. As you look closely at the confession scene, where can you find evidence of the motifs listed in the paragraph above? What are the lessons that can be applied to a minister's or parishioner's life?

3

The Warden

Integrity in the Face of Public Attack

Do it with gentleness and respect, having a good conscience, so that, when you are slandered, those who revile your good behavior in Christ may be put to shame.

1 Peter 3:15–16

*T*he Warden* is an early Trollope novel and the first of an eventual six novels known as the Chronicles of Barsetshire. To understand the story, we need to comprehend some key terms in the novel. The position of warden in this story is akin to what today we might call a chaplain. We are not given many glimpses of the daily duties of the warden Rev. Harding, who also chants the liturgy on Sunday mornings in the local cathedral. We infer that the warden keeps an eye on the physical and spiritual needs of the twelve retirees.

In addition, the term *hospital* in this novel does not refer to a medical facility. It is instead a house or dormitory built in 1434 by John Hiram for twelve bedesmen—retired craftsmen who would pray for their benefactor after his death. John Hiram also built an adjacent house for the warden, whose position also included that of precentor (chanter) at the local cathedral.

The story paints a recognizable picture of a certain strain of Anglican clergyman still evident in England today. At the heart of that image is the institutional Church of England, portrayed more as part of the English social fabric than a spiritual reality. As we progress through the novel, we move in a world of Anglican church positions—bishop, rector, archdeacon, precentor, dean, warden. To be a clergyman is to adhere to the protocol of this institutional framework. The closest we come to a religious experience beyond its institutional manifestations is a two-sentence speech by Rev. Harding to his twelve charges on the evening before his departure from the hospital.

Author: Anthony Trollope (1815–82)

Nationality: English

Date of first publication: 1855

Approximate number of pages: varies with edition from 240 to 285

Available editions: Oxford, Penguin, Modern Library

Genres: clerical novel, Victorian novel, regional writing, Church of England fiction

Setting for the story: the fictional English cathedral town of Barchester, "a quiet town in the West of England," in the 1850s

Main characters: Rev. Septimus Harding, a cleric who serves as "warden" (a minor church position) of an almshouse for twelve needy old men; John Bold, a young surgeon in Barchester who initiates a public crusade to curtail Rev. Harding's moderately lucrative annual salary of 800 pounds; Archdeacon Theophilus Grantly of Barchester, who strenuously defends the right of Rev. Harding to his salary

Plot summary: Hiram Hospital, of which Rev. Harding serves as warden or chaplain, is actually a charity house for twelve destitute retired craftsmen in their declining years. Founded in the fifteenth century, the hospital is supported by an endowment that by the mid-nineteenth century has become prosperous, resulting in a "posh" position for the warden. The benefits include a beautiful quaint house, minimal clerical duties, and an annual salary of 800 pounds. The fiery reformer John Bold sets into motion a public assault on this clerical living, and Theophilus Grantly, the archdefender of Anglican church traditions, takes up the case against the reformers. Rev. Harding, acute of conscience, finally resigns his position and ends his days in an exceedingly humble church position and modest lifestyle.

The mainspring of the action is taken straight from a situation that was unfolding at the very time Trollope wrote the novel. In fact, the opening pages read almost like a journalistic documentary on contemporary events. The situation is as follows.

As the centuries after John Hiram's establishment of the almshouse have unfolded, the estates that serve as an endowment for the hospital have become increasingly prosperous. The initial charter had stipulated that the twelve retirees would have their basic needs met, with the remaining annual income going to the position of the warden. As the estates thrived, the warden's salary grew.

At the beginning of the story, the sixty-year-old Rev. Harding lives free of charge in a picturesque house, with an annual salary of 800 pounds in addition to the 80 pounds for his clerical position as precentor at the cathedral—and all of this for the minimal task of keeping tabs on the twelve old men. Rev. Harding had landed what the narrator calls "one of the most coveted of the snug clerical sinecures attached to our church." The warden's salary, while comfortable, is never portrayed as extravagant. In fact, when Rev. Harding resigns his position, he has no accumulated nest egg.

So the most we can say is that Rev. Harding is the beneficiary of a privileged situation. The so-called reformers who crusade against this privileged situation seem to exaggerate its benefits. It is also important to note that after these reformers have harried Rev. Harding from his position, everyone ends up a loser. The twelve bedesmen lose the added money per day that Rev. Harding had given them out of his own pocket. The position of warden remains vacant, so the twelve have no one to be what Rev. Harding had been to them—"a master, a neighbour, and a friend." As the bedesmen die off, their places are not filled. The warden's house and garden are in total decay. The hospital itself is "disordered and ugly."

A story as firmly embedded in a specific English historical situation as described above runs the risk of seeming unrelated to life today. But literature always uses the particular as a way of portraying the universal. *The Warden* becomes a window to our own world when we identify the issues in ministry that are embodied in the particulars of clerical life in a Victorian village. The remainder of this chapter will explore those issues.

The structure of the story flows directly from the controversy outlined above. Rev. Harding's comfortable life at the story's opening is what occasions John Bold's public crusade. Archdeacon Grantly aggressively defends the church's right to perpetuate the current arrangement. Rev. Harding is caught in the middle of these opposed forces. His need to choose followed by his eventual choice organizes the story.

The Institutionalizing of the Faith

The Warden is a very English book, and the Christian faith is accordingly portrayed as it sometimes appears in the Church of England to this day. The entire religious life that we experience in the novel is expressed in terms of the church and its clerical positions. Virtually the only genuine spiritual note in the entire novel is sounded in Rev. Harding's two-sentence farewell to his charges in the penultimate chapter of the book.

It is difficult to know what the spiritual state of the villagers is or the degree of their knowledge of the Christian faith. We read about worship services at the cathedral, and villagers attend them as the expected thing to do. Above all, religion in the novel is what the clerical guild does and decides. One can pick up the same flavor in some Church of England circles today.

In such a world, preserving the long-standing traditions of the institutional church naturally becomes a clerical preoccupation. In this novel, we see such traditionalism in its pure form in Archdeacon Grantly and to a lesser extent his father the bishop. From start to finish, the unpleasantly assertive archdeacon mounts impressive (if knee-jerk) arguments supporting the church's prerogative to maintain the warden's salary. Archdeacon Grantly's overbearing personality makes him an unsympathetic spokesman for his viewpoint, but in view of how everyone ends up in a worse situation after the reformers have carried the day, a sober assessment might actually credit the archdeacon's defense of the status quo as a worthy position.

For Reflection or Discussion

Assimilating this novel is a good avenue toward experiencing what it means to translate the Christian religion into institutional forms. Perhaps this is a distinctively English situation, but perhaps it is not. We can profitably analyze the forms that this syndrome takes in our own church context. What institutional "scaffolding" have you experienced or observed in mainline or older denominations? What is positive and negative about churches and denominations in which institutional presence is a dominant ingredient? What have you observed regarding the role of the clergy in perpetuating the church as an institution and its effect on the laity?

The Minister's Life Made Easy

A second aspect of the clerical life as portrayed in *The Warden* is closely akin to the institutionalizing of the faith, and again it may appear in heightened form in England and in denominations where much of the minister's duties consists of reading liturgies. The situation in view is a minister's life as an easy life exempt from strenuous spiritual service to people in need. Most evangelical ministers are so overworked that they may find it hard to resonate with what is portrayed in Trollope's novel, but before we reach that conclusion, we need to assimilate what the novel portrays and then ponder possible manifestations in our own situation.

We can begin with the warden himself. His "parish" consists of twelve retired men. Looking after them can hardly put much of a crimp in the warden's daily schedule. We read that even Rev. Harding's admirers "cannot say that he was ever an industrious man; the circumstances of his life have not called on him to be so." Rev. Harding likes his quaint house and garden, but his real passion is music. He has published a lavish collection of ancient church music, he has raised the quality of the cathedral choir, and he plays the violoncello daily for anyone who cares to listen.

The laxity becomes even more pronounced when we turn to the bishop, who according to the narrator "was somewhat inclined to an idle life." He turns the running of the diocese over to his son the archdeacon and spends his time entertaining the clergy of the diocese and their wives. At the end of the story, after the disgraced Rev. Harding has been reduced to a relatively impoverished state, the bishop invites him over for dinner nearly every day, "which means going to the [bishop's] palace at three and remaining till ten"— a seven-hour block.

No one can accuse the bishop's son, the archdeacon, of being inactive, especially when it comes to keeping the institutional machinery running smoothly. But when he enters his study to prepare his sermon, he locks the door, throws himself into an easy chair in front of the fireplace, and reads the semiscandalous fiction writer Rabelais for an hour or two.

FOR REFLECTION OR DISCUSSION

Literature silhouettes the issues it presents with heightened clarity. With that in mind, the depiction of clerical minimalism in Trollope's novel can hardly be irrelevant. To begin, one does not need to be a minister to have pockets of laxity in one's professional or personal life. What are common manifestations of this syndrome in your life or the lives of acquaintances? Similarly, while a minister who spends more time pursuing a passion for music than discharging the duties of a minister may exist only in Trollope's novel, the amount of time a minister allots to his or her personal passions and avocations is a live issue in most ministers' lives. How much time spent in personal interests is legitimate?

Clerical Privilege

Clerical privilege is what drives the plot in *The Warden*. The things that constitute the privileged state of the warden have been noted above: a free house with a garden, a job description that leaves more time for leisure than work on most days, and an annual salary that is moderately large.

We are also given pictures of clerical privilege beyond Rev. Harding. The bishop lives in what is called a "palace," and his job description is vague. His son the archdeacon is the workhorse of the diocese, and he certainly "earns his keep." Yet the rectory, called Plumstead Episcopi, is brimming with a luxury that matches the archdeacon's ambition to be successful. The narrator says of the house that "everything there was of the very best." Both the bishop and the archdeacon are said by the narrator to be "rich."

One of the subtle and profound points the novel raises is embodied in how the clergymen and their friends respond to these clerical perks. Until John Bold fans the flames of public criticism, Rev. Harding "never felt any compunction" in regard to his situation. Once public opposition arises, he has titanic struggles of conscience about it, and in the process, he moves from being a moral nonentity to being a moral hero.

Also relevant are the responses from others when Rev. Harding resigns from the warden's position. Rev. Harding rises to heroic status in the grace with which he accepts the cutbacks and downsizing of his house, income, and church position. But the other privileged ones—bishop, archdeacon, lawyer—are dumbfounded as to how the warden can possibly face the prospect of living on such drastically reduced means. We are left to infer that an inner strength empowered Rev. Harding to accept his reduced lifestyle, as the novel does not spell out the dynamics.

For Reflection or Discussion

The phenomenon of clerical privilege and perks is part of most ministers' lives in some form, and Trollope's novel can serve as a catalyst to thinking about the matter. Most ministers are probably underpaid, but increasingly we hear of ministers' salaries and living arrangements that stagger us. How much is good for a minister? In addition to salary, there is a whole spectrum of things that a beloved minister receives that ordinary people, perhaps living on the same income or less, do not receive. At what point should a minister begin to question the propriety of these things?

Coping with Public Criticism

One of the most contemporary dimensions of the novel is the way in which the practices and clergy of the church are subjected to attack in the public square. The assault begins with a solitary reformer who is eager to uncover possible misconduct in the church. In the novel, this reformer is John Bold, a rabble-rouser who convinces the bedesmen that they have been shortchanged. Of course, the twelve retirees sign the mandatory petition for correction of what they have been swayed to believe exists.

Even more contemporary is the way in which the press gets ahold of the story. The "press" is initially the London newspaper the *Jupiter*, but the story spills over to the Victorian equivalent of magazines or tabloids. Even when John Bold wants to halt the crusade, he is powerless to stop the steamroller of scandal-mongering represented by the London press.

Of course, the scandal seekers exaggerate the facts of the case. For example, one magazine "opened with a scene in a clergyman's house. Every luxury to be purchased by wealth was described as being there." Even details that might be considered factual are given a spin that makes them appear abusive.

The story of the warden's struggle to keep his public image intact is perhaps the most pathetic plotline in the story. When Rev. Harding first considers resigning, it is less out of conviction that his salary is excessive than out of sheer weariness in being publicly attacked. To render the situation even more complex, the warden's friends regard the resignation as an act of cowardice and a defaulting on obligations to the future of the church.

As in real life, the minister in the novel cannot control what happens in the public arena. Thus, the novel poses the question of how a minister can best cope with criticisms that swirl about him.

FOR REFLECTION OR DISCUSSION

The function of literature is to give form to our own experiences. Every minister's fear of public exposure and attack is projected onto the story of the warden's browbeating by reformers and scandal-mongers, with the press as their most powerful weapon. As we read the novel, we can thus contemplate our own situation. Multiple questions arise: what can a minister with integrity do when details of clerical or church life are exposed to public view with destructive intent? What is gained and lost by a minister's escaping from public controversy, as the warden does? Under what circumstances is it appropriate for ministers or Christians generally to defend themselves when criticized in public?

The Minister as Exemplar of Integrity

It is obvious that *The Warden* is a rich repository of issues in ministry. But it also projects a memorable image of the minister in the portrait of the warden. The more we ponder his character, the richer and more sympathetic he becomes.

Rev. Harding begins the story as something of a weakling. The main ingredients have been noted above: a plush salary in exchange for a lightweight workload; spending more time on the avocation of music than the vocation of ministry; never questioning whether a comfortable lifestyle is defensible; mismanagement or naiveté regarding money (despite his free house and income, Rev. Harding "is always more or less in debt to his son-in-law," Archdeacon Grantly); a readiness to toss in the towel regarding the salary dispute, not on principle but because of cowardice in the face of controversy.

But strength of character is seen in a person's ability to transcend initial weakness. Irish poet William Butler Yeats famously theorized, "Why should we honor those who die on the field of battle? A man may show as reckless a courage in entering into the abyss of himself." Rev. Harding looks into the abyss of his weakness and conquers it. Two chief avenues exist for tracing the warden's heroism.

One is the hero's relationship to his unmarried daughter Eleanor (who is in a romantic relationship with her father's nemesis, John Bold). There is no more endearing portrait of a father-daughter relationship in English literature than this one. In fact, the nobility of Rev. Harding might be chiefly seen in the loyalty he elicits from his daughter.

Also important is the story of Rev. Harding's growing conviction that his large salary is unwarranted. That story begins almost immediately after John Bold and the reformers begin their attack. Thereafter it keeps growing, and the warden's integrity becomes progressively grand as it grows. By the time the warden resigns, the opposition from church supporters to the resignation is perhaps fiercer than the attacks from the liberal crusaders had been. In addition to his courage in obeying the voice of personal conscience (when legally he would have won the battle to retain his salary), Rev. Harding's heroism is seen in the grace with which he accepts a demotion in position, income, and lifestyle.

For Reflection or Discussion

For American readers, the setting of the story in Victorian England, along with the Anglican trappings of the church situation, might make the story seem remote from contemporary life. But with the picture of the minister as hero we move into the realm of the timeless (with the accompanying quality of being perpetually up-to-date). In what ways is Rev. Harding a heroic character? What edification does that portrait yield for both ministers and laypeople?

4

Elmer Gantry

The Travesty of an Almost-Christian

If I were still trying to please man, I would not be a servant of Christ.

Galatians 1:10

For Sinclair Lewis, and a generation of readers familiar with his work, the name "Elmer Gantry" is synonymous with hypocrisy. In fact, in American culture, Elmer Gantry has become a byword for a huckster or religious charlatan. And if one peruses recent Southern fiction, especially that in which religious professionals feature prominently, it is easy to see the reflection of Elmer Gantry in many a character.

The novel is primarily intended as a character study of its protagonist, Rev. Elmer Gantry. As such, the plot proceeds episodically rather than sequentially. The reader is therefore provided with a series of vignettes, arranged more or less chronologically, which reveal the moral sentiments and religious outlook of its central figure.

As the story unfolds, we follow a recognizable career path from a young man's conversion in college to a minister with national recognition. The novel falls into four parts: (1) Gantry's college days, conversion, and calling to the ministry (chaps. 1–5); (2) his seminary education, ordination, and first church internship (chaps. 6–10); (3) his collaboration with Sharon Faulkner on her evangelistic crusades (chaps. 11–15); and (4) his embrace of New Thought and Methodism, his growing prominence as a minister and social reformer, and his narrow escape from being publicly exposed as a hypocrite (chaps. 16–32).

Even though Lewis directs his lampoon at charlatans like Elmer Gantry, he is clearly interested in satirizing American fundamentalism as a whole. In fact, Lewis reveals his intentions at the outset when he dedicates his novel to

Author: Sinclair Lewis (1885–1951)

Nationality: American

Date of first publication: 1927

Approximate number of pages: 420

Available editions: Signet, Penguin, Dell

Genres: novel, character study, Southern fiction, satire

Setting for the story: Midwest, small-town, fundamentalist America in the first half of the twentieth century

Main characters: Elmer Gantry, the protagonist; Jim Lefferts, his best friend in college; Lulu Bains, Gantry's girlfriend at the church of his first internship; Dr. Zechlin, Elmer's brilliant, agnostic seminary professor; Sharon Faulkner, the traveling evangelist with whom Gantry collaborates; Cleo Benham, Elmer's wife; T. J. Rigg, a criminal lawyer in Zenith; Hettie Dowler, Elmer's personal assistant and mistress who conspires to expose him publicly

Plot summary: The novel follows the career trajectory of Elmer Gantry from his conversion in college to his establishment as a minister with national recognition. The opening chapters recount Elmer's college career, conversion, and call to ministry. This is followed by his seminary education, ordination, and first ministerial internship, which comes to an abrupt end as a result of a scandalous sexual affair he has with a church member, Lulu Bains. After this debacle, Elmer finds refuge from the temptations of ministry as a traveling salesman for the Pequot Farm Implement Company. But after two years, he craves the limelight of ministry and thus seeks to return to ministry. Gantry's open door comes when he joins the team of a well-known traveling evangelist named Sharon Faulkner, who becomes his colleague and lover. This professional and romantic relationship continues for Elmer until, one evening at a gospel crusade, a fire envelops the meeting place and takes Sharon's life. In the fourth and longest part of the novel, Gantry ascends to a place of prominence as a minister and social reformer. The novel concludes dramatically with Gantry nearly being publicly humiliated and exposed for his extramarital affair with his personal assistant.

the prominent social critic H. L. Mencken, who was very outspoken about his distaste for fundamentalism. And while Lewis is not quite as scathing, he obviously shares Mencken's aversion to that brand of religious faith and practice.

Because the novel is sarcastic and at times uncharitable, some will be tempted to dismiss it as too lopsided to be helpful. Hence the urge to brush aside its characterizations and implied critiques as a cheap parody rather than an incisive portrait of reality. But this would be to miss the salutary benefits of reading it.

Despite its largely unsympathetic and even belittling descriptions of religious life in American fundamentalism, the novel provides what we may view as a

Christian critique of Christianity, not unlike what we find in the prophetic tradition of the Old Testament. Sometimes the only cure for religious hypocrisy is mockery, since nothing else will be heard.

The Christian reader can learn from Lewis's probing character study of Rev. Elmer Gantry, for who is altogether free of the sins that so easily entangle a person? Who is not tempted in similar ways? Who is free of those little vices that Elmer displays rather prominently? Or which church, or denomination, is not able to turn (albeit inadvertently) the Christian faith into a commodity to be traded, a product to be marketed?

Let the one who is without sin be the first to cast a stone. And in the meantime, let us turn to *Elmer Gantry* and allow the travesty of an almost-Christian to have a sobering and humbling effect upon our souls. For while Rev. Elmer Gantry is not very good, he is not altogether bad. He is, instead, human—all too human.

The Drug of Oratory

We first meet Elmer Gantry in college, and by all accounts he is a most unlikely candidate for the Christian ministry. He is a football star and in fact an "authentic idol of the college." But he is also a rabble-rouser, a miscreant, a womanizer, and a boozer. That is why his classmates call him "Hell Cat." Evidently this is a young man with little interest in intellectual attainments, the cultivation of character, or improving the lot of others. Instead, he is preoccupied with lesser things.

What, then, draws Elmer into ministry? And, equally interesting, what keeps him there? Lewis's answer is a simple one, even though he develops it over the course of the entire novel. Elmer is addicted to praise; he is hooked on "the drug of oratory." And it just so happens that among the various professions, the Christian ministry is best suited to keep the hits coming.

While in college, Elmer is first introduced to the pleasure of possessing an audience. There is his public speaking class, which certainly develops his longing for praise. But on one occasion Elmer finds himself thrust into the middle of a crowd and is almost caught off guard by how good it makes him feel. The people's gaze is a bonfire; Elmer warms his hands in their rapt attention. And just as heat when applied to an object causes expansion, so, too, Elmer expands in the warmth of adulation.

This and similar experiences shape Elmer's decision to enter ministry. At first he does not want anything to do with Christian service, despite the cajoling of nearly everyone in the college, who recognize him as a "win" for the kingdom of God. Elmer himself acknowledges that the life of a minister certainly has advantages: good social standing, adoring congregants, and plenty of leisure time to ponder those "highfalutin ideas." But entering the ministry also means making a few painful sacrifices: in particular, no more drinking or flirting with women, two diversions that do much to disrupt the monotony of life.

As Gantry wrestles with indecision, the prospect of praise provides the catalyst to move him beyond the impasse. He fantasizes about holding an audience, playing it as though it were an instrument and he a musician. "To move people—Golly!" Elmer reflects enthusiastically. "He wanted to be addressing somebody on something right now, and being applauded!" Thus, he makes his decision, and into the ministry he goes.

And to Elmer's surprise, his first church internship, undertaken while he is in seminary at Mizpah, does not disappoint. Elmer finds the little church to which he is assigned more impressive than he would have imagined. Even a small congregation, assembled in his honor, "their attention flowing into him and swelling him," makes him feel quite "healthy, proud, expansive." In fact, he can't help but self-assuredly encourage himself with the thought, "Lemme at that pulpit!"

Later his craving for more and more praise inspires him to join forces with a popular traveling evangelist named Sharon Faulkner. Elmer is convinced that this is a sure path to endless applause, the thought of which gratifies him more than the titillation he otherwise receives from the usual suspects: smoking cigars, drinking booze, chasing women. And Gantry is right: those were glorious days on the road with Sharon. As her lover and as a member of her entourage, Elmer had everything he desired: "his girl, his work, his fame, his power over people." What more could anyone want?

The addictive power of praise draws Elmer into ministry and later back into ministry. Yet, tragically, it also keeps him from reforming his ways while in ministry. At one particularly significant juncture during his ministry with Sharon Faulkner, Elmer flirts with the idea of changing his ways. In fact, he contemplates ending his rebellion and praying for complete deliverance from his vices.

But in the end, he cannot follow through. For one thing, he knows it will be impossible to keep either Sharon or himself away from the invigorating melodrama of evangelistic crusades. Furthermore, he is simply too "exalted by his own oratory" to ever forsake it. How could he? The addiction is real; he must go on ministering.

For Reflection or Discussion

Lewis's exploration of the effect of praise upon the psyche is one of the more powerful contributions of the book; it is also one that ought to give pause to anyone who makes a living by speaking. What are some indicators that one is developing an addiction to praise? How can one be shielded from its allure? How can we respond to praise in ways that promote humility rather than pride?

The Center of the Universe

If narcissism is an unhealthy preoccupation with oneself, then Rev. Elmer Gantry is certainly a narcissist. In fact, the various species of Elmer's narcissism appear at virtually every turn. Early on we are told in a matter-of-fact way, "Elmer assumed that he was the center of the universe and that the rest of the system was valuable only as it afforded him help and pleasure." The remainder of the novel serves to flesh this out in a most depressingly colorful way.

During the Sharon Faulkner years, for example, his evangelistic preaching is simply riddled with self. Gantry's debut performance with Sharon's gospel crew, in which he is featured as the speaker for the night, is a case in point. In that sermon, Gantry extols the virtues he himself had displayed in his own decision "to let Jesus save him," as he put it. This was a well-suited turn of phrase and preparation for the close of his message, as he speaks to all the sinners who are present: "Won't you come?" he pleads. "Won't you help me? Oh, come! Come down and let me shake your hand!" And when they do, several dozen, in fact, weeping as they come, Elmer himself weeps; indeed, he "wept at his own goodness."

Elmer's placement of himself at the center of the universe leads him to exploit others, often rather shamelessly. Like many of the flaws in his character, this one, too, is evident already in college. There Gantry is known as someone who is always demanding things of others: "He wanted everything." Friends, to say nothing of acquaintances or even strangers, are to Elmer but pawns on a chessboard, to be moved around according to his good pleasure.

Using others for his own ends characterizes even his most intimate relationships. The cold and calculated deceit he displays in his relationship with his girlfriend Lulu Bains is enough to turn the stomach of a sensitive reader. Yet we see the same mode of operation with his own wife, Cleo Benham. In fact, it is clear that Elmer cannot help but interpret the whole of his domestic existence in terms of himself. Evidently wanting to drive home this point, Lewis devotes a number of pages to exploring, indeed, exposing, the hypocrisy of his home life, not least in the way he treats his children.

However, one of the ironies with a narcissist like Elmer Gantry is this: while such a person feeds on others, he often feels at the same time isolated from others, bereft of genuine relationships. Narcissists seldom have true friends. Elmer certainly does not. Even Jim Lefferts, Elmer's college buddy and only real friend, is in the end driven away by Elmer's opportunism when Elmer decides, much to Jim's chagrin, to get saved at the YMCA crusade. Jim is a skeptic and cautions Elmer about getting carried away by the religious fervor of such an event. Elmer does not listen but is instead overtaken by the urging of the crowd and the special pleading of the evangelist. It all seems splendidly right at the moment. Even though Elmer knows this decision means being false to Jim, still he kneels that evening in confession before others. To be sure, his words of confession—even his will to confess—are not so much his own as the crowd's. Regardless, Elmer now knows "the rapture of salvation—yes, and of being the center of interest in the crowd."

Elmer Gantry is therefore a lonely soul. Loneliness dogs him wherever he goes: he is lonely in college, lonely after his conversion, lonely in seminary, lonely on his wedding day, and lonely in his later years. This is the narcissist's paradox; this is Elmer Gantry's dilemma. He is the center of his universe yet inconsolably lonely there.

FOR REFLECTION OR DISCUSSION

It is often said that the Christian ministry is a lonely calling. Why do you suspect that is? When have you felt the loneliest in ministry, and how have you responded? What did your loneliness reveal about your motivations for ministry and the quality of your relationships? In what ways does your ministry get in the way of good relationships? How might your desire for control hinder genuine relationships?

A Professional Good Man

For Lewis, Rev. Elmer Gantry is more than a religious charlatan or huckster. He is also the quintessential religious professional. He is the consummate "professional good man." He is a thoroughgoing pragmatist in all things religious, from education to denominational allegiances, spiritual experience, the selection of a spouse, and even the rearing of children.

What becomes clear in all this is that Lewis has little patience for the anti-intellectualism he perceives within American fundamentalism. The novel contains any number of shots at what he regards to be its intellectual barrenness and superficiality, its penchant for clichés and well-worn slogans. We are told, for example, that the faculty at Mizpah Theological Seminary, where Elmer attends, is too "scholarly" and "learned" to do anything other than spend "the rest of their lives reading fifteenth-hand opinions, taking pleasant naps, and drooling out to yawning students the anemic and wordy bookishness which they called learning." Reinforcing this criticism from the opposite direction are Lewis's sympathetic portraits of agnostics within the fold, seminarians like Frank Shallard and professors like Dr. Zechlin, who have enough intellectual integrity and honesty actually to wrestle with their questions rather than paper over them, something Lewis applauds.

Arguably, Lewis's chief concern is with the utilitarian approach to learning characteristic of American fundamentalism, which itself stems from a professionalized view of the ministry. If the ministry is simply a profession, then everything about the ministry is professionalized. For the minister, then, the only question becomes, how will this promote, or impede, the advancement of my ministerial career? Or to put it even more crassly, what's the cash value of this?

Elmer approaches not only his ministry preparation but also the entire execution of ministry in a spirit of professionalism. We are told, for example, that Elmer finds seminary education even more boring than undergraduate education. The only thing that keeps him going (besides the occasional diversions of the city of Monarch) is the credential of the bachelor of divinity degree, which in his estimation symbolizes professional perfection. Learning for its own sake, of course, is beside the point. What Elmer covets is instead the kind of training that makes one an effective professional—what is useful for good sermons and raising money and keeping congregants contented.

Elmer has little patience for the rigors of serious theological education. That is why he finds Dr. Zechlin's enthusiasm for Hebrew syntax annoying, not to mention the fact that the learned professor offers "no useful tips for ambitious young professional prophets." Alternatively, Elmer cheerfully imbibes nearly everything Dean Trosper has to offer in his courses on practical theology and homiletics. This is because in the dean's class Elmer and his fellow students receive proper instruction in the really critical issues of ministry: "what to say when they called on the sick, how to avoid being compromised by choir-singers, how to remember edifying or laugh-trapping anecdotes by cataloging them, how to prepare sermons when they had nothing to say, in what books they could find the best predigested sermon-outlines, and, most useful of all, how to raise money."

One of the few benefits of seminary training from Elmer's point of view is that it puts him in possession of a whole new vocabulary. He now has not only a vast array of fine-sounding theological terms at his disposal but also dozens of stock phrases for nearly every occasion. Thus, in a conversation with, say, an old, humble farmer, Elmer can proudly display all the really deep stuff he knows: "hermeneutics, chrestomathy, pericopes, exegesis, homiletics, liturgics, isagogics, Greek and Hebrew and Aramaic, hymnology, apologetics—oh, a good deal."

Naturally, Elmer's professionalized approach to education carries over into his approach to every other aspect of ministerial life, from evangelistic preaching to denominational politics. Quite telling is Elmer's first sermon as a new member of Sharon Faulkner's evangelistic crusade. It is a cloudburst, a huge success. We read that it has "structure as well as barytone melody, choice words, fascinating anecdotes, select sentiment, chaste point of view, and resolute piety." Most importantly, it traced a theme he knows well, one he believes in with all his heart: "the cash value of Christianity."

Elmer even approaches marriage this way—in terms of its cash value. Gantry is not really attracted to his wife, Cleo Benham, yet he is convinced that she is just the sort of wife who will help advance his ministerial career and who will even help him capture a bishopric! Elmer also understands his piety and character in professional terms: "Virtue, he pointed out, certainly did pay."

Indeed, the gospel itself becomes a commodity that Elmer markets, advertises, and even sells. In fact, this is just what Elmer seeks to do: "Oh, I'm not buying—I'm just selling—selling the gospel!" Elmer has a knack for advertising and thus benefits from the "salesmanship of salvation." The advent of the typewriter, in particular, is a real boon for Elmer because his entrepreneurial spirit had been cramped by the inefficiencies of pen and ink. A keyboard enables his advertising impulses to gallop. Gantry also carefully cultivates relationships with the local newspapers. In fact, no other ministers are "so hearty, so friendly, so brotherly." Elmer understands the importance of good publicity if one is really committed to growing a church.

Elmer also knows how to spruce up weekly church services and draw bigger crowds. While in Zenith, he perfects the art of Sunday services: in the morning service, he gives people the "solid religious meat" they need to get through the week; in the evening service, he gives them something a little lighter, more novel, and a whole lot tastier—what Gantry calls sermon "cream puffs." Predictably, his Sunday evening services are a real success because of his fine knack for inventing "stunts" to attract the crowds and, as he likes to say, "wake them up."

In short, Rev. Elmer Gantry's entire outlook on the ministerial profession fits hand-in-glove with the spirit of the age and the needs of the hour. This is something Sinclair Lewis underscores: "He was a professional. As an actor enjoyed grease-paint and call-boards and stacks of scenery, so Elmer had the affection of familiarity for the details of his profession—hymn books, communion service, training the choir, watching the Ladies' Aid grow, the drama of coming from the mysteries of back-stage, so unknown and fascinating to the audience, to the limelight of the waiting congregation."

FOR REFLECTION OR DISCUSSION

How would you define the difference between ministry as a calling and ministry as a career? Why is it so easy to succumb to professionalization in our approach to ministry? Where do you see signs of the professionalization of the Christian ministry or ministry education and training?

The Limits of Self-Reformation

There is no denying that Elmer Gantry is a rather off-putting character. Especially for those with sincere moral sentiments or religious commitments, the temptation is to dismiss Gantry as too over-the-top to be useful except to be dismissed. But that would fail to do justice to the subtlety and complexity of his person. It would also fail to appreciate that underneath the obvious vices with which Gantry struggles are deeper and deadlier idolatries with which we all struggle.

In the final analysis, Gantry is not simply a womanizing religious phony. He certainly struggles with that, but he is not merely that. In fact, his spiritual pathology is not primarily lust or greed, those so-called animal appetites. Instead, his vices are vanity and pride, the more spiritual of the vices, and the ones of which none of us is entirely free.

We need to appreciate an element of complexity in Elmer Gantry's character. Behind the pasty façade of self-serving religiosity we catch an occasional glimpse of something genuine, something real, something authentic. Elmer is not simply a fictitious parody of what is real. There is a human element to him, and this is the very thing that makes his character so tragic: he is the consummate almost-Christian.

At one level, we see a kind of moral improvement insofar as his commitment to career advancement within the church compels him to get a better grip on his more obvious vices: boozing, carousing with women, and the like. He knows this is one of the challenges of entering the ministry: no more of his delightful little diversions. And, to some extent, he succeeds in this effort. He is able to get "victory over his lower nature." However, this means exchanging a lesser vice for a greater one—subduing lust by animating vanity and pride. Thus, in the end, Gantry turns out to be twice as much a "Hell Cat" as he was in college.

Elmer Gantry is like a man struggling to wake from a deep sleep but to no avail. Despite his best intentions, he cannot escape the slumber of his unregenerate state. As a result, his entire life and career are compromised. He makes resolutions to reform his ways, and the effort seems real enough at the time. Yet in the end his moral reforms are ephemeral, like some exotic dream, for Gantry lacks the will to find the way. Therein lies the travesty of Rev. Elmer Gantry, and of every other almost-Christian.

For Reflection or Discussion

Where do you see the most hypocrisy in ministry? In what areas of life or ministry are you most tempted to be a hypocrite? How do we tend to simply replace lesser vices with greater ones? And what does Elmer's being an almost-Christian say to you about the state of the Christian church and the Christian ministry today?

5

Witch Wood

Powers and Principalities in Flesh and Blood

For we do not wrestle against flesh and blood, but against the rulers, against the authorities, against the cosmic powers over this present darkness, against the spiritual forces of evil in the heavenly places.

Ephesians 6:12

In 1642, the Church of Scotland entered into a Solemn League and Covenant with the English Parliament, uniting both countries under the banner of Presbyterianism. The following years were epochal for England and Scotland. As Oliver Cromwell's Puritan army waged war against the House of Stuart, Scotland's James Graham of Montrose sought to rally supporters to the Catholic cause.

All of this forms the political, military, and theological backdrop for John Buchan's *Witch Wood*, a novel of dark hypocrisy and spiritual warfare. Buchan's portrait of Scottish Presbyterianism is partly a caricature. Yet as a literary work, *Witch Wood* tells a masterful tale of godliness in conflict with wickedness. In the year 1644, Buchan's protagonist takes charge of the parish of Woodilee, near the bewitching Black Wood of Melanudrigill.

Innocence Turns to Experience

Woodilee is David Sempill's first (and only) parish, and he begins his ministry in the full flush of youthful enthusiasm. Buchan's novel is partly an exploration of how a young preacher's idealism gets chastened by the hardships of

Author: John Buchan (1875–1940)

Nationality: Scottish

Date of first publication: 1927

Approximate number of pages: 380

Available edition: Replica Books, a division of Baker & Taylor

Genres: historical fiction, pastoral romance, magic and suspense, gothic, story of innocence and experience

Setting for the story: the rural parish of Woodilee during the 1640s, when Presbyterian hopes of uniting England and Scotland were threatened by James Graham of Montrose. The nearby Black Wood of Melanudrigill serves as a foreboding setting for deeds of devilish evil but also as a pastoral setting for natural beauty and romantic love.

Main characters: David Sempill, an idealistic young Presbyterian minister in his first pastoral charge. Other characters include ministers from the local presbytery; a motley crew of saints and sinners from the parish, including his chief antagonist, Ephraim Caird; and Katrine Yester, the daughter of a noble house who becomes the love of his life. One of Montrose's leading soldiers (Mark Kerr) becomes the minister's staunchest ally in contending against the witchcraft in Woodilee.

Plot summary: Young David Sempill takes charge of Woodilee and begins preaching and caring for people in spiritual and physical need. Yet the Black Wood of Melanudrigill casts a dark, mysterious shadow on Reverend Sempill and his ministry. He discovers why on Beltane's Eve, when members of his parish (in disguise) offer pagan sacrifices and hold demonic revels in the wood. The minister's righteous, jealous, and sometimes angry efforts to expose the perpetrators divide the parish and arouse the antagonism of his church elders, who prove to be the ringleaders of the local coven. Meanwhile, another conflict is taking place within Sempill's own soul as he seeks to reconcile his calling as a minister with the fatal hypocrisy he sees in the Church of Scotland and with his own passion for natural beauty and human freedom, as personified by the fair, innocent Katrine Yester. Sempill's enemies discredit his ministry and bring him up on charges before the presbytery, leaving him with a choice between remaining true to his calling and escaping with Katrine. The minister's choice causes him to lose his parish of Woodilee and the woman he loves but also gives him one final opportunity to confront demonic evil.

ministry, with the changes that result in his character and his understanding of his calling.

Few pastors embark with larger zeal or higher hopes than David Sempill. Buchan describes him singing on his way from Edinburgh to Woodilee, praying as he reaches the threshold of the manse, and weeping with gratitude when he first sits down in his study. The minister's great ambition is to be a faithful servant, saving and comforting the immortal souls God has placed in his charge. As the new minister gazes at Woodilee from a nearby hillside, his heart tenderly yearns for the little flock God has appointed him to feed.

Sempill's first summons to pastoral duty, at a farmhouse deathbed, fills his heart with pious gratitude and a benediction of peace. Soon the young minister engages in the full range of pastoral duties: studying the Bible, preaching a series of sermons on "the fourfold state of man" (a detail drawn from the life of the famous Scottish preacher Thomas Boston), catechizing local children in the manse kitchen, and doing relief work among the helpless poor, especially during the winter storms. Sempill has a heart for living with his people in their "daily wrestling for life." "For a man o' God," the people say, with evident affection, he's "like a plain body."

As he exercises these ministrations, Sempill has an exultant assurance of his vocation. Yet he also has a naively idealistic view of ministry in the church—an idealism that will soon become chastened by hard experience. In addition to having high spiritual expectations for his parishioners, Sempill begins his pastorate with blind confidence in the wider kirk and its shining mission of righteousness. He has equally grand ambitions for his own progress against ungodliness. But as one of his allies later observes, "You see the ills of the land and make haste to redd them, but you have no great notion of what is possible."

The list of Sempill's disappointments in ministry is lengthy. His sermons sometimes fall on deaf ears as his parishioners, with their "frozen decorum," sit in stony silence. He finds it virtually impossible to lead people to repentance for sin. He gradually gives up his hope of producing the great scholarly work he had hoped to write on Isaiah. He finds himself ill-equipped to succor the dying or save them from damnation. The charge of Woodilee lies heavy on his soul, and on one occasion he is tempted to flee the parish and forsake his calling. Perhaps most disappointingly of all, he is forced to confess the deep unworthiness resulting from his own sins: blind fear, rash anger, and general faithlessness in the service of God. What he sees at presbytery only adds to his disillusionment. In the end, therefore, he suffers "the ruin of those high hopes with which a year ago he had begun his ministry."

As the novel traces these (maybe inevitable) disappointments, it shows a corresponding growth in the young minister's wisdom and godliness, as well as his understanding of Christ's call to ministry. *Witch Wood* is a story of sanctification in which the reader is invited to observe and reflect on the spiritual progress that may come when innocence turns to experience. For David Sempill, this progress comes in Christlike compassion, discernment, gentleness, and courage, especially in his life-or-death confrontation with the powers of evil.

Where do you see the biggest disparity between what you hoped your ministry in the church would be and what it actually is? Reflect on your own experience since first beginning to fulfill your calling in the church. What were some of the memorable joys of your first duties in ministry? How has your understanding of your calling changed since you began serving Christ? How has your character developed?

The Minister Girds Up His Loins

From his first encounter with the dark wood near Woodilee, Sempill senses that Melanudrigill is a locus for wickedness. As a natural setting, the wood is described as a place of unhallowed gloom and impenetrable darkness. Sempill knows he should not fear anything in the world that God has created. Yet the minister is frightened nonetheless by the heathen wood and its black secrets.

As the novel unfolds, it becomes apparent that the wood itself is not the heart of Woodilee's darkness. When seen by daylight, and when inhabited by the fair lady Katrine Yester, the wood takes on a brighter aspect. "It is a blessed and innocent place," she says. The true darkness of Melanudrigill—what makes it a stronghold for the devil—is human depravity, especially the corruption of false religion. As an extended and deliberately ambiguous metaphor, the wood symbolizes the duality of the human heart.

A master of suspense, Buchan uses the dark mystery of the wood to create a sense of impending evil. The minister gradually comes to believe that the devil has chosen to make the miserable parish his own, because the depravity he encounters there is not mere sinfulness but out-and-out wickedness. As he undertakes his pastoral responsibilities, he discovers ever-widening circles of iniquity.

The first signs of sin are various forms of godless superstition that the minister encounters in the parish—things that had "no warrant from the Bible." More alarmingly, there is a rash of births out of wedlock, mostly stillborn, with the sinister suggestion that this is an annual occurrence. Soon Sempill witnesses the shameful truth: some of his church members secretly go into the wood on the eve of certain feast days to celebrate pagan and demonic revels. To make matters worse, the leaders of this devilry include elders of his own kirk.

The sin of this black witchcraft is compounded by the hypocrisy it fosters. The minister does not know who all the participants are, but whoever they are, they continue to attend public worship, employ pious expressions in their everyday conversation, and quote him a good deal of Scripture. The novelist thus uses an extreme form of evil—witchcraft—to expose the more common but equally deadly sin of hypocrisy: the gap between true godliness and the mere profession of religion. The people of Woodilee are living a lie. "Who can I trust?" the minister asks. "The man who is loudest in his profession may be exulting in secret and dreadful evil."

Things are just as bad in the presbytery, which refuses to deal with the sin of Woodilee's elders and turns on their minister instead. The leaders of the presbytery are "blind fools that call themselves ministers of God," and their sins are legion: Pharisaism, theological hairsplitting, a judgmental spirit, the tyrannical abuse of church discipline, the miscarriage of justice, and the perversion of Calvinism by presumption on the doctrine of election ("this demented twist of John Calvin that blasts and rots a man's heart"). Buchan also imputes to the pastors and elders of the kirk the sin of driving ordinary people into "the nethermost works of darkness." By the end of the novel, these works will include a communal witch hunt that culminates in sacrificing a woman to Satan. Yet his chief elder assures him that it has all been done "decently and in order" (see 1 Cor. 14:40).

How should a minister respond to this "superfluity of naughtiness"? David Sempill is ordained to wage spiritual warfare against "the Powers of the Air" and "the Principalities of Darkness." His allies beg him to proceed cautiously, at first by trying to keep him far away from the wood and later by encouraging him to let his preaching bring evildoers to repentance. "Trust to your grand Gospel preachin', Mr. David," his housekeeper counsels him. The local blacksmith gives similar advice: "Let it alone, sir. . . . Have patience, sir. . . . Trust in the Word, while it is your duty to preach, to bring conviction of sin in the Lord's ain gude time, for the arm o' flesh will fail ye."

Whether or not this is wise counsel is left for the reader to decide, but the minister chooses to follow a more combative approach. On Beltane's Eve, when he chances upon strange figures dancing to the devil's piping, he rebukes them with "the fury of an Israelitish prophet." Afterward, Sempill vows not to rest until he has "rooted this evil thing from Woodilee" by "the terror of God and the arm of the human law." To do any less is to fail in his first duty to his parish and his calling as a minister of the gospel.

In waging war against the dark powers of the wood and of Woodilee, Sempill believes that his spiritual battle is also a struggle with flesh and blood. The figures who attacked him in the wood were not demons but human emissaries of the devil. Thus, his strategy for combating evil is both practical and spiritual. With the help of local farmers who do not want to see a brave man go down to defeat, he executes a bold scheme to reveal the identities of the revelers in the wood. When provoked, he draws his sword.

Yet the minister also employs the spiritual weapons of prayer, the sacraments, and the Word of God. As a soldier of the Lord, he can combat the devil only "by the spirit of God and such weapons as God has expressly ordained." Sempill declares that there will be no sacrament of communion until there has been a general confession of witchcraft and other sins. As a stimulus to repentance, he confronts his leading elder with a personal accusation of sin. He also preaches against hypocrisy with righteous anger, tempered at times with tears of pity. He calls down "the terrors of the Most High" against the priests of Baal in Woodilee and pleads with "poor deluded sinners" to abase themselves before the mercy seat. The minister also takes his case to the courts of the presbytery (unadvisedly, as it turns out), which has the power of spiritual discipline.

How effective is Sempill's practice of physical and spiritual warfare? "There's maybe better ways o' guidin' it," one skeptical farmer says when he hears how the minister intends to confront the revelers in the wood. Yet Sempill's strategy is largely vindicated by the events that follow. He sees the fight through to the end and fulfills his vow to "lay bare the evil mysteries of the Wood."

If the minister has a fault, however, it is the impatience of his crusading zeal. When Sempill vows not only to unveil the wickedness of Woodilee but also to "blast its practitioners into penitence" and "scorch them into salvation," his wrath is not altogether righteous. Indeed, as he later admits, his anger is partly driven by his own terror of the wood. Sempill's anger sometimes gets the best of him, as he is "carried outside of himself in his fury." As a man of action, his growing admiration for men like the ancient prophets, who fought with deeds as well as words, makes him increasingly restless in his calling as a minister of the gospel. Buchan's portrayal of evil in the church thus reveals some of the perils that may befall those who are brave enough to fight against it.

For Reflection or Discussion

David Sempill confronts moral evil in several of its most reprehensible manifestations. In what ministry situations have you been most aware of being engaged in spiritual warfare—knowing that, as Paul said, your fight is not with flesh and blood but with principalities and powers? What are some of the ways you have encountered hypocrisy in the church? How have you confronted it, and how effective have your efforts been? What are some of the most valuable lessons you have learned from contending against evil in the course of ministry?

The Counterblast

The wickedness in Woodilee has one further manifestation that merits separate mention because of its prevalence in pastoral ministry. Because of his commitment to combat evil in all its forms, Sempill comes under direct and personal attack from people in both his parish and his presbytery. This opposition, or "counterblast," as Buchan calls it, requires the minister to learn how to respond when his ministry is under assault.

The most blatant form of opposition is the physical attack Sempill suffers in the wood when members of his flock, operating incognito, leave him bruised and battered. But this is far from the most painful wound the minister receives. Once he blasts the parish by publicly denouncing its witchcraft, his parishioners turn a deaf ear to his ministry of the Word. People avoid him in the street, averting their eyes. Things are equally bad at the presbytery, where his fellow ministers rail at him, entertain fanciful charges brought against him by his own elders, and suspend him from the duties of his calling. As the opposition mounts, Sempill becomes the scapegoat for the plague that befalls the village. Finally, the presbytery adds insult to injury by deposing him from the ministry and excommunicating him from the church. The novel thus portrays various forms of opposition to a man's ministry: criticism, ostracism, and blame.

Not all of Sempill's responses to his opponents are commendable. His flagging commitment to the standards of the wider kirk and its doctrines of divine judgment seems out of step with his calling. In refusing to vacate his pulpit (as the clerk of the presbytery requests and recommends), he is well within his rights. Nevertheless, the manner of his refusal is high-handed. At other times the accumulated weight of discouragement tempts Sempill to abandon his work as a pastor. Indeed, there are hints throughout the novel that he has mistaken his true calling, that the man inside the minister is better suited to the life of a layman, possibly a soldier. This tension partly stems from some of Buchan's misrepresentations of the ministry as a contemplative calling that operates in a spiritual realm without engaging the fullness of human life—a false dichotomy between nature and grace. Still, Sempill's struggle with this dilemma helps readers clarify the true calling of a minister, or any servant of Christ.

What enables Sempill to persevere in his calling—until it is taken away from him—is the vow he has taken to fulfill his ministry as a servant of Christ. Nowhere is his commitment to the pastorate more evident than in his perseverance in the face of opposition. Sempill meets every attack with a display of godly virtue. His fury against the evildoers in his own parish turns to compassion when he comprehends the extent to which they have been seduced by Satan. His obvious affection for his people wins many of their hearts, as love will do. His parishioners know he has always had "the kind word and the open hand to puir folk," especially in times of trouble, and when they look back on his ministry, they will long remember him as a preacher of charity. At least, some of his people will remember him that way. Making a clear allusion to the ministry of Jesus Christ, the narrator avers that although Sempill had "the publican and sinners" on his side, "the Pharisees and scribes were against him."

The minister's anger toward the scribes and Pharisees of the presbytery is also transformed, turning to meekness. As his ecclesiastical trial progresses, he finds the grace to explain his actions honestly, not defensively, and in humility to submit to his eventual censure. Since Sempill's alleged misdeeds are really acts of mercy, he suffers for the sake of righteousness.

Sempill is ready to go even further. In his passion to save his people's souls from perdition, he is willing to be cast away himself. He proves this at the end of the novel when he loves his archenemy among the elders (Ephraim Caird) dearly enough to drag him into the bewitching wood and compel him to make his final choice between God and the devil, between salvation and damnation. In his flesh-and-blood battle against the powers and principalities of evil, David Sempill sanctifies the wood by making it a place where Christlike love is sacrificed for the ungodly.

For Reflection or Discussion

Witch Wood *is partly the story of a conflict between a minister and his congregation. What are some of the ways your own ministry has come under personal attack? What were some of your best and worst reactions? What did you learn about how to respond to criticism and about the ways God wants you to grow more into the likeness of Christ?*

6

Murder in the Cathedral

The Minister as Martyr

The good shepherd lays down his life for the sheep.

John 10:11

Murder in the Cathedral was a solicited composition. During the 1930s, a group known as the Friends of Canterbury Cathedral organized an annual festival of performing arts to raise money to support and beautify the cathedral. Originally the festival sponsored existing plays from the past by such towering figures as Alfred, Lord Tennyson; John Masefield; and Lawrence Binyon. In 1935, the group requested an original play from T. S. Eliot, who was followed by such notables as Charles Williams and Dorothy Sayers.

Eliot turned for his story material to Thomas à Becket, a famous martyr from English ecclesiastical history who was murdered in 1170 in the cathedral a mere fifty yards from the chapter house where the play was first performed. Although Becket is the main character in the play, he is not the only hero of the story.

Eliot embodies his Christian message by telling two stories simultaneously. One is the story of the archbishop's progress toward martyrdom. The first half of the play presents the temptation of the hero in which Becket is tempted first to escape the martyrdom and then to accept it for selfish reasons. In the second half of the play, Becket endures martyrdom as an exemplary saint. Together these two events embody the Christian experience of suffering for Christ's sake.

The protagonists of the second story are the poor women of Canterbury, who speak in unison as a chorus (a technique borrowed from ancient Greek

Author: Thomas Stearns Eliot (1888–1965)

Nationality: American born; English by elected citizenship

Date of first publication: 1935

Approximate number of pages: 90

Available edition: Harcourt Brace Jovanovich

Genres: poetic drama, martyr's life, saint's life, historical fiction

Setting for the story: Canterbury, England, in December of 1170

Main characters: Thomas à Becket, Archbishop of Canterbury under King Henry II; a chorus, consisting of the poor women of Canterbury; three priests of the cathedral who function as Becket's confidants; four tempters of Becket who in some productions "double" as the four knights who murder him

Plot summary: The historical context of the action is King Henry II's power struggle with Thomas à Becket for supremacy in England. In the first half of the play, Thomas wrestles with the question of whether he should avoid martyrdom by abandoning his pattern of advancing the interests of the church over the king's political interests, and also with the question of how, if he accepts the martyrdom, he can do so from selfless motives. The wrestling takes the form of four tempters who appear before Thomas. In the second half of the play, with the internal struggle now over, Thomas courageously endures martyrdom. He can do so because he perceives that the unfolding process that will lead to his martyrdom has been the catalyst to the spiritual progress of the chorus. A second main action is thus the chorus's coming to salvation after beginning in a state of complete spiritual apathy.

tragedy). Step-by-step, we can chart the spiritual progress of the chorus, from initial spiritual lethargy to eventual belief in Christ as Savior. Eliot presents salvation by showing its operation in the consciousness of the chorus. The actions performed by the archbishop—the cleric in the story—are the initiating factor in the spiritual progress of the chorus (his congregation). In this way, the play becomes a case study in how a pastor can influence his followers—and in turn how these followers can play a crucial role in the spiritual formation of their shepherd.

The Temptation of the Minister

In the first half of the play, the protagonist wrestles with the growing threat to his life posed by the hostility of the king. Thomas à Becket had been Lord Chancellor, next to the king the most powerful political figure in England. When he later became Archbishop of Canterbury, head of the church in England, he gave precedence to the church over the state. A collision of wills between king and archbishop ensued.

Eliot's way of dramatizing the need for Thomas to come to grips within himself over the possibility of martyrdom involves four tempters who appear before Thomas and interact with him. The first three tempt Thomas to avoid the martyrdom, respectively by (1) returning to the carefree life of his youth, before he became a political figure (personal escapism); (2) returning to political favor with the king by abandoning his loyalty to the church (escape from religious duty); and (3) siding with the rising political power of the country lords (advancing the church's cause through an alliance with political power). Eliot presents these three temptations in terms of a time sequence—past, present, and future, respectively.

The fourth temptation is subtler, consisting of the temptation to accept the martyrdom for self-seeking reasons—doing the right thing for the wrong reason. This is the most intense temptation because it touches the motivations of the heart that no one else can see. Three reasons for accepting martyrdom are stated: (1) the earthly glory that comes to a martyr; (2) the heavenly glory that a martyr receives; (3) the satisfaction of revenge on one's enemies as they suffer in hell. To confirm that this is the most intense temptation, Eliot has Becket say at different points, "I have thought of these things," and, "Who are you, tempting me with my own desires?"

FOR REFLECTION OR DISCUSSION

The story of Thomas in the first half of the play poses the issue of a minister's needing to decide what course to follow when faced with external threat from hostile powers. What forms does such threat take in your own life? What compromises are you tempted to make when confronted with threats to your person or ministry? How can you do the right thing for a wrong reason? If you are a minister, what are some of the right things in your ministry that you are tempted to do for wrong reasons?

"The Small Folk Drawn into the Pattern of Fate"

The role of the chorus is to demonstrate the progress of faith in the "small folk" of Canterbury. In each of the main speeches of the chorus, we can trace spiritual progress. The first choral speech displays the complete spiritual indifference of the chorus, summarized in the statement, "We are content if we are left alone." But the women of Canterbury have fears and intuitions that "some malady is coming upon us" (a reference to the growing threat to their archbishop), something that would represent "disturbance of the quiet seasons."

In subsequent speeches, the members of the chorus increasingly acknowledge the presence of evil in society and in themselves. The chorus speaks ironically (as it often does) when it requests, "Leave us to perish in quiet." The import of that statement is that the women will perish spiritually if allowed to continue on their course, although at this stage the women wish only to die (perish) in their complacency. Near the midpoint of the play, the chorus utters a speech acknowledging an evil that is interior to them, "flowing in at the ear and the mouth and the eye."

But the role of the chorus is more extensive than dramatizing the growth of the soul toward salvation. The chorus represents (in its own words) "the small folk drawn into the pattern of fate." What this means is that the chorus plays an essential role in the spiritual development of Thomas. In the first half of the play, this takes the following form: after the departure of the fourth tempter, Thomas is at an impasse. His two options are to abandon his religious duty by avoiding martyrdom or to accept it for self-aggrandizing reasons.

Faced with this impasse, Thomas remains silent as the members of the chorus express their growing consciousness of evil in themselves. As the chorus ends the speech, the women say (speaking "truer" than they know), "Save us, save us, save yourself, that we may be saved." The women are thinking at the level of physical safety; Thomas sees a spiritual meaning in the word *save*. He responds by blurting out, "Now is my way clear, now is the meaning plain." In other words, having seen the spiritual progress of the chorus, Thomas sees the possibility of embracing martyrdom as a means of bringing the chorus to a state of complete spiritual salvation.

For Reflection or Discussion

A good avenue toward interpreting the action in the first half of the play is to trace the effect that Thomas and the chorus have on each other as the danger to Thomas's life intensifies. How does the threat to Thomas show the women the evil that requires their conversion? How does the spiritual progress of Thomas's congregation lead to his own spiritual progress? How have you seen pastors and their churches influence one another for spiritual good?

"For the Glory of God and for the Salvation of Men"

Right in the middle of the play Eliot inserted a Christmas Day sermon preached by Thomas (one of just two prose passages in the play). The ostensible theme of the sermon is the paradox involved in celebrating the sacrament of communion—Christ's death—on the same day that Christians celebrate Christ's birth. But within the context of this particular play, the function of the sermon is to establish an interpretive commentary on the unfolding action.

At this point, we need to remind ourselves of the double plot of the story, since statements in the sermon apply to both plots. One is the story of the death of a martyr. The other is the chorus's coming to faith. With that double plot in mind, here are four key statements that can be applied to the protagonist of the play, or the chorus, or both:

1. "It is only in these our Christian mysteries that we can rejoice and mourn at once for the same reason."
2. "We rejoice, that another soul is numbered among the Saints in Heaven, for the glory of God and for the salvation of men."
3. "A Christian martyrdom is never an accident, for Saints are not made by accident."
4. "A martyrdom is always the design of God, for His love of men, to warn them and to lead them, to bring them back to His ways."

The sermon (based on historical records) that Eliot inserted into the middle of the play is a foreshadowing of what is to come, but it is equally a passage to which we should return after assimilating the entire play.

FOR REFLECTION OR DISCUSSION

In Thomas's Christmas Day sermon, Eliot becomes a travel guide to the meaning of his play. What statements in the sermon apply to Thomas himself as a Christian martyr? What statements clarify the effect of that martyrdom on the chorus? How do both of these aspects add to our understanding of the vocation of the pastor and his relationship to his church?

"For the Glory of God": The Minister as Heroic Martyr

The first half of the play features Thomas's internal struggles regarding his impending martyrdom. In the second half, Thomas encounters the external combat with the soldiers who murder him. Eliot built upon the historical data that had been passed down through history. One of these details was Thomas's refusal to bar the door of the cathedral. Another was his commending himself and his cause to God as the knights were about to kill him.

As the martyrdom becomes more and more inevitable, we can see the spiritual courage of Thomas growing. Along the way, he utters some memorable statements, made all the more luminous by their context in the ongoing action of the play. Here are four statements worthy of pondering:

1. "Death will come only when I am worthy. . . . I have therefore only to make perfect my will."

2. "I have had a tremour of bliss, a wink of heaven . . . ; all things proceed to a joyful consummation."
3. "I give my life to the Law of God above the Law of man."
4. "Now is the triumph of the Cross."

As we ponder these memorable statements, we can profitably analyze how they contribute to our understanding of Eliot's protagonist and also the Christian worldview Eliot embodied in his play.

Eliot gives a full picture of spiritual heroism in his portrait of Thomas. What specific details make up this picture of an ideal spiritual shepherd? According to the action in the second half of the play, what spiritual resources are available to someone who is marching to his or her own death out of loyalty to Christ? How does the example of Thomas serve as a model as you contemplate your own death?

"The Salvation of Men": The Redemption of the Congregation

The subplot of the chorus's spiritual progress continues systematically as the second half of the play unfolds. The stages of that progress include the chorus's full conviction of its own fallen state and need for cleansing; a vision of hell as God's judgment against evil; and a psalm of praise to God (in confirmation of the statement of the chorus early in the play that "we are forced to bear witness," which turns out to mean bear witness to their faith in God). The death of Thomas is an atoning death—not in the sense that it is the basis of the chorus's salvation but in the sense that Thomas is willing to endure martyrdom because it is the event that leads the chorus all the way to saving faith.

In keeping with the intertwining stories of Thomas and his congregation, more is going on than the salvation of the members of the chorus from their sins. A main action of the second half of the play is creating in the lives of the onlookers an attitude of acceptance of the efficacy of the martyrdom. But if Thomas's priestly colleagues and congregation must come to an understanding of what his martyrdom accomplished, so must the audience, and therein lies Eliot's most daring move of all.

In the second prose passage in the play, the four knights who have just killed the archbishop step forward and address the audience. They offer a series of explanations for their actions that on the surface make perfect sense—so much so that only by conscious effort can we refute them. As all the commentators agree, this is the temptation of the audience, something that is even clearer when (as in the very first performance of the play) the same actors who play the four tempters in part 1 play the roles of the four knights in part 2. Three key arguments emerge as the knights congratulate one another on their allegedly brilliant ideas: (1) the knights were "completely disinterested" and did not derive any personal reward for their murder of Thomas; (2) modern people who accept as an axiom that church and state should be separate cannot help but approve of the knights' actions, which were after all an assertion of "just subordination of the pretensions of the Church to the welfare of the State"; (3) Thomas could have avoided the martyrdom, and the fact that he did not proves that his death was in effect a suicide.

The "third priest" rises to heroic status as he speaks for us in countering the seemingly plausible arguments of the knights. The kernel of his speech is this:

> No. For the Church is stronger for this action,
> Triumphant in adversity. It is fortified
> By persecution: supreme, so long as men will die for it.

A speech like this (along with others late in the play) is a device of disclosure by which Eliot shows how he wants us to interpret the action.

FOR REFLECTION OR DISCUSSION

Answering the following questions will unfold the meanings of the second half of the play. What are the stages through which the chorus moves en route to achieving a state of salvation? How is that process affected by the willingness of their spiritual leader to endure death for his faith (in confirmation of a key statement by Thomas that his murderers "shall find the shepherd here" [that is, in the cathedral] and that as a result "the flock shall be spared")? Casting a retrospective look over the play as a whole, what can we learn about the following issues in ministry: (1) the temptation to run from duty in the face of opposition and potential harm; (2) the hypocrisy of doing the right thing for selfish reasons; (3) renunciation of self as the path of service and glory; (4) ways in which a faithful pastor can influence a congregation; and (5) the personal qualities of character required of pastors who aspire to be models to their churches?

7

The Diary of a Country Priest

The Power of an Ordinary Ministry

Blessed are the poor in spirit, for theirs is the kingdom of heaven.

Matthew 5:3

he Diary of a Country Priest is a magnificent story about the power
of an ordinary ministry. The narrative revolves around the fictional
diary of a young curate who describes the daily ministrations of his
first parish and his response to them. Set in the rural village of Ambricourt,
France, in the 1930s, the narrative traces the steady physical decline of this
young priest through a series of events and interactions that open up new
layers of complexity in his circumstances and inner life.

The narrative itself advances almost entirely through the protagonist's
own diary entries. This creates the impression of a close proximity between
the reader and the narrated events, whether they be encounters with others
or the priest's own ponderings. This literary strategy invites the reader to
engage with the unhappy events, physical demise, and emotional anguish of
the protagonist as he carries out his ministerial responsibilities. As a result,
the book offers the reader candid insights into some of the difficulties of a
minister's life.

It is worth acknowledging at the outset that reading Georges Bernanos's
Diary of a Country Priest is not for the faint of heart. While it is an immensely
rich and rewarding read, the tone of the novel is grave, its mood dreary, and
its pace slow, even at times tedious. For example, in the opening pages, Bernanos sets the scene for what ensues with two melancholy images: drizzling
rain and dust. The reader is then told, through the voice of the priest, that
these symbolize the boredom that eats up his own parish, as it does the entire
world. Not without good reason, then, did Graham Greene, one of the other

Author: Georges Bernanos (1888–1948)

Nationality: French

Date of first publication: 1937

Approximate number of pages: 300

Available edition: Carroll & Graf Publishers

Genres: novel, Catholic novel, saint's life, fictional diary

Setting for the story: Ambricourt, a rural village in France, during the 1930s

Main characters: the young curate of Ambricourt, who remains unnamed; the priest of Torcy, a tough-dealing man who is also the curate's mentor; Madame Pégriot, the curate's housekeeper; the young girl Séraphita Dumouchel, who seems to enjoy mocking the curate during his catechism class; the countess, Madame Comtesse, hardened because of the untimely death of her child, yet in the end finds peace with God; the countess's daughter, Chantal; Madame Louise, Chantal's governess who first solicits the curate's assistance with the family's personal matters; Doctor Delbende, the village doctor and a committed atheist; Louis Dufréty, the curate's seminary friend in whose house he dies

Plot summary: The narrative revolves around the fictional diary of the young curate and describes both his inner life and his daily ministrations of his first parish, concluding with his untimely death. Unprepared for the realities of parish ministry in rural France, the curate arrives in Ambricourt with high hopes for his ministry. These are quickly dashed as the reality of life in the village sets in. Despite his best efforts, he becomes the subject of village gossip and the object of much ridicule and suspicion. His difficulties are exacerbated due to the decline in his health, the visible signs of which cause some in the parish to express disdain for him. The central episode and high point of the novel comes when the curate gets involved in the personal lives of the most prestigious family in the village and is instrumental in the mother of the family, Madame Comtesse, turning back to God after many years of bitterness and unbelief. As his health continues to decline rapidly, the curate eventually discovers he is afflicted with stomach cancer. The novel closes with the young priest lying on his deathbed in a friend's home, away from his own parish, acknowledging the pervasive presence of grace.

great Catholic novelists of the twentieth century, compare Bernanos's stories to open wounds that refuse to heal.

One can trace the novel's movement along two inversely related lines or trajectories: one follows the slow physical demise of the priest, culminating eventually in his untimely death; the other follows his ever-increasing resignation to the will and ways of God, climaxing in his dying words, the oft-quoted and triumphant closing lines of the novel: "What does it matter? Grace is everywhere."

While this dual movement within the narrative creates a certain tension, it also enables its author to make one of his more profound theological contributions. In fact, one could describe Bernanos's *Diary of a Country Priest* as his own extended literary reflection on the paradoxical reality of Christian life and ministry, captured by the apostle Paul in his well-known words from 2 Corinthians: "So we do not lose heart. Though our outer self is wasting away, our inner self is being renewed day by day" (4:16).

Because of this conception of Christian experience, the novel serves as a powerful antidote to idealized conceptions of Christian life and ministry. It also serves as a forceful critique of genteel forms of Christianity. Evidently Bernanos, like Luther, had little patience for corruption within the church. In fact, Bernanos's *Diary* can be viewed as his own protestation against the scandals of the institutional church, a church overtaken, in his estimation, with boredom. As the protagonist-priest says in the novel's opening pages—and here one suspects he speaks directly for the author himself—the boredom of the institutional church is "an aborted despair, a shameful form of despair in some way like the fermentation of a Christianity in decay."

Bernanos's *Diary* can be classified within the literary genre known as the Catholic novel. This genre was developed in the late nineteenth and early twentieth centuries in reaction to the Enlightenment's explicitly secular and antireligious bias. Champions of this genre included Charles Péguy, François Mauriac, Graham Greene, and Bernanos himself. These novelists were for the thinking Catholics of that era what Dorothy Sayers, T. S. Eliot, and C. S. Lewis were for the intellectually engaged Anglicans of that same period.

The Catholic novel as a genre was defined by the presence of several closely related themes. First, the redemption of the sinner was the central message of Christianity; second, mystical substitution was the means of divine redemption; third, there was an implied critique of materialism; and, fourth, there was an implied celebration of God's tireless pursuit of the erring soul. Each of these themes is found in Bernanos's *Diary of a Country Priest*, and together they serve the Catholic novel's chief aim: to advocate for an incarnate Christianity in the face of a spiritualized church and a materialized world.

The Diary of a Country Priest thus provides the reader not only with an example par excellence of the Catholic novel but also with a compelling Christian vision of the world and how life ought to be lived in it. Bernanos portrays ordinary existence in a way that is fully embodied and yet deeply theological at the same time. He is able to bring together in a coherent vision what we are so often tempted to see as at odds in life and ministry: the grief of human experience and the grace of God. Yet only insofar as we appreciate the way in which Bernanos comingles these two very ordinary realities—human suffering and divine kindness—can we experience the truly challenging and edifying effect of his story.

"A Friend Made in My Image"

Despite his daily interactions with members of his parish, the young curate nevertheless remains friendless. In fact, the vast majority of his relationships are filled with misunderstanding and suspicion, condescension and meanness. Even the parish children, whose affection he admits he longs to receive, scorn him with their childish tricks. After one particularly naughty prank, he laments, "Children are children—but, oh, why should these little girls be so full of enmity?"

On another occasion he receives an unsigned note in his letter box that reads, "A well-wisher advises you to apply for a change of parish. And the sooner the better. When at last you open your eyes to what everyone else can see so plain, you'll sweat blood! Sorry for you but we say again: 'Get out!'" These are snapshots of the relational wilderness the priest inhabits. As he says at one particularly low point in the story, "My solitude is complete and hateful." His parish has become his Garden of Gethsemane, and his isolation mirrors Christ's own.

However, in the midst of his isolation, the priest seeks companionship and a measure of consolation in his diary. In fact, for him his diary is "a friend made in his image," the "only friend with whom I still manage to speak openly." Throughout the story, then, he interacts with his diary as if it were a distinct presence, a person to whom he can turn for a sympathetic ear and thus unburden his agonizing soul.

Interestingly, the reader witnesses his diary return the favor; his diary becomes itself a voice that talks back to him. And while this provides the priest with the relational intimacy he craves, it presents him with another complication and, as a result, a new source of insecurity: is the dialogue nothing more than a monologue? Is he simply caught inside his own head? This niggling doubt explains why he expresses hesitancy from the beginning with keeping a diary and why he resolves to do so for only twelve months, as an experiment, and then to toss its pages into the fire and forget the whole thing.

The priest is clear about the purpose of his diary: it is to enable him to see himself more clearly and thus come to terms with the impact he's having—for better or worse—on those under his care, the members of his parish. "This diary is of immense help," he says at one point, "in forcing me to see my own share of responsibility in so much bitter disappointment." By putting his own inner life on paper, he is able to attain greater self-awareness and a more thorough understanding of who he is and who he is not. Furthermore, the blunt reality of a written record of his reactions to experiences and events helps curb any drift toward self-deception. Thus, the reader is offered an entrée into the subtle relationship between self-understanding and self-delusion: "Who am I?" versus "Who do I perceive myself to be?"

One of the functions of the diary is to allow the priest to confront the reality of who he is. Why is having a correct self-understanding so important in life and ministry? In what ways are we prone to delude ourselves? How can we counteract these tendencies?

"A Very Commonplace, Very Ordinary Man"

North American culture has been called narcissistic. Narcissism is a trait many of us share. We are preoccupied with ourselves. Ironically, however, our fixation with ourselves introduces a host of psychological ambiguities and tensions into our lives. On the one hand, we relish rather grandiose visions of who we are; we have a robust sense of our own self-worth, human potential, and innate goodness. On the other hand, we often find ourselves crushed under the weight of our own foibles and failings and sometimes bored to the point of despair by the dullness of our own existence. Our inflated sense of self has a hard time coming to terms with the remarkably ordinary realities all around us as well as within us. This is the tension with which many of us live. More than that, this is a burden under which many of us suffer.

In this light, we can say that even though the young priest is intensely interested in his own interior life, he is so in a very un-narcissistic way. He exudes a startling humility; he is remarkably circumspect about who he is, not only in relation to his God but also in relation to his parishioners. He recognizes that his life is but a run-of-the-mill life, or as he says of his experiences, they are "the very simple trivial secrets of a very ordinary kind of life." No delusions of grandeur here.

Yet this is precisely where the young curate finds profound freedom: embracing his own ordinariness, his own nothingness. For only by so doing does his perception of himself mirror the reality about himself, and therein he discovers the key to liberation. He knows his life is ordinary, and indeed, ordinary it is. He also anticipates an ordinary death, and ordinary it is. "My death is here," he recognizes. "A death like any other, and I shall enter into it with the feelings of a very commonplace, very ordinary man."

This sober estimation of himself, in turn, shapes his approach to his daily ministrations within his parish. Control tempts every minister. Yet the priest of Ambricourt models what it might look like in ministry to relinquish control: whether control of self, control of others, or even control of God. In fact, he consistently resists the temptation to explain the circumstances in his life, much less to rationalize them. Instead, he simply resigns himself to the will of God in an ever-increasing way.

Thus, the young priest of Ambricourt has no desire to be the "master" of his parish. He only longs to embrace the simple fact that he is nothing more than "a pitiful beggar" laboring alongside his people. But therein, again, Bernanos wants his readers to understand, lies the secret to true freedom: the freedom of a child that does not demand, the freedom of innocence that does not presume, the freedom of the kingdom of God that does not seek to control but only to receive.

FOR REFLECTION OR DISCUSSION

The reader is encouraged to view the priest's humility as the product of his intense introspection. Yet when does an interest in one's own interior life become an unhealthy form of narcissism or preoccupation with oneself? How does freedom come from a sense of one's own insignificance?

"Sweet Miracle of Our Empty Hands"

Ironically, the young priest's own suffering and sense of insignificance enable him to serve his parishioners much more effectively. His own brokenness and doubt allow him to open himself to their disillusionment and pain, which prompts them to open themselves in turn to him. On one occasion, a parishioner finds herself in his presence pouring out her bottled-up grief over her mother's death. Later on we hear him reflect upon the conversation: "I didn't want to interrupt her, for I felt sure she had never told so much to anyone before, and she really seemed to be waking suddenly from a dream; she was confused."

One way in which Bernanos highlights the remarkable approach of his protagonist to parish life is by contrasting the priest's youthful innocence and even naiveté with the seasoned and plain-dealing approach of his mentor, the priest of Torcy. "What the church needs is discipline," the priest of Torcy insists. "You've got to set things straight all the day long. You've got to restore order, knowing that disorder will get the upper hand the very next day, because such *is* the order of things, unluckily." Thus, rather than cultivating the theological virtues of faith, hope, and love, the priest of Torcy advises the humanistic triad of control, respect, and obedience.

One of the practical implications of these divergent approaches is their attitude toward transparency and vulnerability. While the priest of Torcy keeps his own trials entirely to himself, concealed under a hard crust of straight talk, the young priest's sufferings are in plain view for everyone to see. Yet as the narrative unfolds, we learn that it is his suffering itself that serves as the platform for his ministry. This leads us to one of the novel's key contributions to our understanding of ministry: Christian ministry is not an expression of the overflow of grace in one's own life; it is, instead, the *pursuit of grace* in one's own suffering and in the suffering of others. As such, our conception of the minister is profoundly reshaped: the minister or parish priest is not ultimately a repository of grace but only a conduit of grace.

Importantly, then, as the young curate seeks to serve his parish with his simple acts of obedience, he recognizes the importance of his daily ministrations as a priest—i.e., catechizing the youth, reciting the Mass, hearing confession—and yet the far greater importance and transformative power of his simple acts of *suffering*. At night, as he lies on his bed, he constantly whispers to himself by way of reminder, "Suffering for the sake of others. Suffering for the sake of others. Suffering for the sake of others." Suffering is, then, not only a requirement of his vocation; it is also the primary means by which he succeeds in the cure of souls. Ministry is sharing in—one might even say, communing with—the pain of others: opening one's self to another's pain, receiving it as one's own, and embracing it. By doing so, the priest is convinced he is following in the footsteps of his Master, who not only shared in our humanity but also bore our burdens.

Integral to this vision of ministry is an understanding of how divine agency is present in and through suffering. This dimension of *The Diary of a Country Priest* is arguably best depicted in the central episode of the novel—the priest's confrontation of the countess, Madame Comtesse. The countess is portrayed as a proud woman, hardened by earthly wealth and privilege. She is also angry and defiant, embittered by the death of her infant son. Her grief is thus mixed with anger and despair, a debilitating combination that has caused her to turn decidedly away from God.

In his weakness, the young priest becomes an instrument of grace and transformation in the life of the countess. Through the course of their tense exchange, the countess finds herself—even despite herself—turning back to God. She then confesses this to him. Reflecting on this later on, the priest provides a beautiful description of the way in which his own human agency played into the countess's conversion: "Oh, miracle—thus to be able to give what we ourselves do not possess, sweet miracle of our empty hands!" Consistent with this, he prays, "Lord, I am stripped bare of all things, as you alone can strip us bare, whose fearful care nothing escapes, nor your terrible love!" As one who possesses nothing in himself save poverty of spirit, he is fit to serve as a conduit, not a repository, of grace. A pitiful beggar going from door to door with outstretched hand—this is the image of the minister we find in Bernanos's *Diary*.

FOR REFLECTION OR DISCUSSION

How do you view your own ministry toward others? Have you tended in the past to view yourself as a conduit or a repository of grace? How does being a conduit of grace transform your view of meeting the needs of others and serving out of weakness and need rather than strength and sufficiency?

"Grace Is Everywhere"

"Does it matter? Grace is everywhere." These are the priest's last words, his dying words; these words also capture the theological vision of the novel as a whole. Yet by the time we arrive at this point in the narrative, we are prepared to affirm that in order for grace to be everywhere, suffering also must be everywhere. In fact, these closing words find counterpoise in an opening line of the novel, where the priest matter-of-factly observes that "good and evil are probably evenly distributed." Suffering is ubiquitous; this we recognize. So is grace, Bernanos insists, even though we have far greater difficulty recognizing it.

The Catholic theologian Hans Urs von Balthasar was of the view that Georges Bernanos surpassed all other Christian writers of modern times in celebrating the reality of the grace of God. Indeed, within the theologically infused world Bernanos creates in his *Diary*, the reality of grace pervades everything, for in the end, the realities of suffering and grace coincide; in fact, one is tempted to say, they *happily collide*—collide, for Bernanos, at least, in the life of the young priest's own cruciform existence.

Thus, the priest's short pilgrimage in his obscure parish patterns itself after Christ's own. And just as the Gospel narratives make no apology for the presence of suffering in the life of Jesus' followers, so Bernanos does not shy away from portraying the priest's own suffering as something not unusual but expected. This is the lot of ordinary human beings.

Yet because suffering is ordinary, so too is grace. Grace is everywhere.

For Reflection or Discussion

In the novel, grace is connected to suffering. This is one of the book's principal theological points. Does this make suffering itself redemptive? And if grace is most often experienced in the midst of affliction, rather than on either side of it, are we to seek suffering so that we can experience grace?

8

The Power and the Glory

Can a Bad Minister Produce Good Fruit?

But we have this treasure in jars of clay, to show that the surpassing power belongs to God and not to us.

2 Corinthians 4:7

In *The Power and the Glory*, Catholic novelist Graham Greene set out to tell a "jar of clay" story in which the extreme unworthiness of the priest makes any positive effect of his ministry a result of God's working rather than human merit. In the background lies Catholic confidence in the efficacy of the church's sacraments and rites in themselves, quite apart from the life of the minister who performs them.

One of the first things to strike the reader is the naturalism of the story. This is a literary term used to denote extreme realism. A story in this tradition focuses relentlessly on the ugliness and misery of life. A strong pessimism and determinism are part of the picture as well. From the buzzards circling overhead in the second sentence of the story to the firing squad's killing of the priest three pages from the end, readers of this novel need to brace themselves for an endless succession of scenes of squalor, poverty, and moral depravity.

This doubtless shows Greene's adherence to the literary tradition known as naturalism, which is simply part of modern literature. But we can also relate it to the religious dimension of the novel: the result of all the sordidness we encounter while reading the novel is that we observe Christianity struggling and persisting in the face of suffering and persecution.

In addition, the story is so deeply rooted in the topography and sociopolitical fabric of a specific locale in southern Mexico that the book quickly emerges as an example of regional writing. How did an English author educated at Oxford University come to write a novel set in such a remote place? A journalist as

Author: Graham Greene (1904–91)

Nationality: English

Date of first publication: 1940

Approximate number of pages: 300 in original edition; 200–240 in later editions

Available edition: Penguin

Genres: novel, Catholic novel, suspense story, adventure story, regional writing, naturalistic novel, saint's life, martyr story

Settings for the story: Chiapas and Tabasco, provinces in the very south of Mexico, during the 1930s

Main characters: A wealth of important secondary characters fill the world of the story, but there are three main actors. The protagonist, never named, is a Catholic priest on the run from governmental agents trying to stamp out Christianity in Mexico. His behavior is often reprehensible, and he is familiarly known as "the whiskey priest" because of his addiction to alcohol. The priest's chief antagonist is the lieutenant of police, a socialist who hates religion. The so-called *mestizo*, a half-Indian peasant, is the Judas figure who betrays the priest to the lieutenant for execution.

Plot summary: As the story opens, the whiskey priest is on the run from the anti-Catholic police "red shirts." As a fugitive, he travels secretly from village to village as a hunted criminal. The priest is a guilt-haunted wanderer, overwhelmed by his sense of personal sinfulness and betrayal of his clerical calling. Yet the priest continues to perform his usual priestly duties of administering communion and baptism in the places he visits in his fugitive journeying. Although the priest lacks the qualities of a conventional martyr, it is clear in the closing pages that the author wishes to place him in that category. As the title of the novel hints, Greene views the priestly office as ultimately efficacious, and we see this chiefly in the positive effect the priest has on various characters in the story, though not in the priest's own spiritual life.

well as a fiction writer, Greene specialized in visiting dangerous places about which he then wrote, including Vietnam, Kenya, Poland, Cuba, and Haiti.

In 1938, Greene was commissioned by his publisher to report on religious persecution in Mexico. What Greene saw was what he put into *The Power and the Glory*. The totalitarian president of Mexico (Plutarco Calles) and the governor of the province of Tabasco (Tomás Canabal) undertook a ruthless campaign to eliminate religion. The number of priests was decimated, churches were closed, and the practice of religion was outlawed. An additional detail important to Greene's novel is that liquor was prohibited. Greene was shocked by the religious persecution he witnessed in Mexico, and so are we as we read *The Power and the Glory*.

The Catholicism portrayed in the novel fits Greene's own religious persuasion. Accordingly, we experience the institutional trappings of Catholicism from the inside as we read *The Power and the Glory*. Everywhere we turn, the Christian faith is portrayed in outward and institutional terms—the saying of Mass, the conducting of baptisms, the hearing of confessions, the kissing of the priest's hands.

Greene divided his story into four parts, and we can see the overall shape of the story in this division. Part 1 introduces us to the general situation of religious persecution and to a gallery of characters with whom the priest will have dealings as the story unfolds. Part 2 narrates the perilous journey of the priest through various locales, ending with his having drifted across the border into a safe province. In part 3, the priest decides to leave the safe province to give dying rites to an American criminal, an action masterminded by the traitorous mestizo to bring about the priest's arrest by the lieutenant (with whom the priest conducts an extended discussion about religion). Part 4 returns to some of the "bystanders" of part 1 but is mainly devoted to the execution of the priest.

The Minister as Sinner

The most obvious trait of the protagonist is his depravity. This is not to say that this theme gets more space in the book than other aspects of the characterization of the priest, but only that it is the thing that leaps out from the pages of the novel. The story is an unfolding litany of clerical failings, seen in the priest's addictions, immorality, cowardice, neglect of clerical duties (or resentful performance of them), and inner awareness of being a scoundrel.

Greene himself labeled the priest "the whiskey priest," and while the priest's addiction to drink is not his only failing, it is a unifying motif in the story. For example, the priest drinks at Mr. Tench's house in the opening scene. He ends up in prison because he is caught with a bottle of contraband brandy in his possession. On the night before his execution, he sits on the floor of his cell drinking the bottle of brandy the lieutenant brought him.

We witness other scandalous behavior in the priest's life as well. He has fathered an illegitimate daughter. He sometimes performs his priestly duties resentfully. He is capable of charging high prices to conduct baptisms.

Scattered throughout the story are brief passages in which the priest reflects on his own awareness of his sinfulness, both personally and professionally. It might be a brief aside that "five years ago he had given way to despair" as a way of life. Or it might be the more extended passage in which the priest recalls his ambitious, success-driven early career as a priest in a successful parish. The priest reflects on his own failings and fear of death the night he spends in prison. On the night before his execution, he concludes to himself that he has "been so useless, useless," and he feels that "he had to go to God empty-handed, with nothing done at all."

The function of the negative portrait of the priest is twofold. On the one hand, we are led to contemplate something we know to exist in real life: a minister whose conduct is reprehensible. But this novel takes that one step further by raising the question of whether a minister's bad behavior cancels out the effectiveness of his ministry.

For Reflection or Discussion

Mastery of this novel requires the reader to trace the thread of the priest's bad behavior. What aspects of the priest's character and conduct are demonstrably immoral? What does the novel say about life by means of this portrait of the priest's failings? How do you reconcile yourself (if at all) to your awareness that ministers are sinners too?

The Priest as Sufferer

Beginning with the story of the patriarch Joseph and extending through the lives of Christ and the apostles in the New Testament, the archetype of the suffering servant embodies much of what biblical faith commends and commands. The suffering servant is someone who undergoes unmerited suffering in order to produce a redemptive effect in the lives of others. The whiskey priest of *The Power and the Glory* fits the archetype.

The priest's most obvious suffering stems from the fact that he is a hunted man whose life is in constant danger. In this regard, the story is a continuous suspense story and adventure story, and Greene does a masterful job of portraying the burden of living with one's life under threat of death every hour of every day. Metaphorically speaking, the priest suffers the anguish of living on death row with an undetermined day of execution. Already at the end of the opening chapter, we hear the priest praying, "Let me be caught soon." A counterbalance to the priest's depravity is his continuing loyalty to his priestly calling, the very thing that makes him a hunted man. He could have escaped long ago if he had chosen to do so.

The priest actually performs numerous acts of virtue and duty to his own disadvantage. In the opening chapter, he misses a boat that would have enabled him to escape to safety when he accompanies a boy to attend his dying mother. He refuses to abandon the mestizo (who is bent on betraying the priest to the civil authorities) when he falls ill. He feels a sense of responsibility for his illegitimate daughter, Brigida, when he visits her village. During his night in a crowded prison, he feels compassion for his fellow inmates. And running through the entire novel is the foil or contrast represented by Padre Jose, a former priest who buckled under the pressure of persecution and resolutely refuses to perform priestly duties for anyone.

The ultimate act of suffering for the faith is martyrdom, and if we pay attention to scattered hints, it is obvious that it was Greene's intention to present the priest as a martyr. The seed is planted as early as the prison scene, in which a woman declares, "We have a martyr here." The priest passes it off with a giggle, but the motif has been planted in our minds.

At the end of the story, the priest could have remained safe if he had not ventured across the border into unsafe territory to administer last rites to a dying gangster. Late in the story, as the pious mother reads the hagiological story of the martyr Juan to her children, Luis asks regarding "the one who stayed with us that time" (i.e., the whiskey priest) whether "he was one of the martyrs of the Church," and the mother says yes.

Like the protagonist in T. S. Eliot's hagiological play *Murder in the Cathedral*, the priest emerges as a Christ figure. He dies an atoning death that is efficacious in the spiritual lives of others. The gangster to whom the priest is lured by his "Judas" is named James Calver, a name that evokes "Calvary." As a traveling man hunted by religious opponents who wish his death, the priest is repeatedly ministered to by followers who feed and house him.

The minister in this novel is someone who suffers. As hostility to Christianity around the world grows, Greene's novel is more relevant with every passing year.

For Reflection or Discussion

On a first reading, it is easy to see only the priest's depravity. But on subsequent readings, the counter to that emerges. It is important, therefore, to keep our antennae up for evidences of the priest's status as a suffering servant. In what ways does the priest suffer? What is Greene saying through this spectacle of suffering? How does the priest's suffering become a paradigm of every Christian's calling and experience in a fallen world?

The Priest as Hero

To assert the heroism of the whiskey priest might seem initially to be a hard case to make. After all, it is the failings of the priest that the novel highlights. But there can be little doubt that it was the author's intention partly to idealize the priest and present him as a heroic figure. If we dig deeply enough below the surface of the priest's failings, we can find a bedrock of clerical heroism. This heroism is seen chiefly (but not exclusively) in the lives that are positively influenced by the priest.

To see this, we can profitably start with the final scene of the book. The lieutenant who oversees the execution of the whiskey priest walks away from the execution scene smug in his assumption that he has silenced Catholic religion in his province. But in the middle of the night, a priest arrives secretly in the village and knocks at the door of a Catholic family. A little boy named Luis opens the door and eagerly kisses the hands of the stranger. Who is this boy? He is the son of a pious mother who earlier in the story had displayed indifference when his mother read the story of an exemplary martyr named Juan. In fact, Luis had admired the lieutenant for his machismo. But the boy who heard about the priest's execution now spits on the lieutenant's pistol and embraces the faith of the newly arrived priest.

Or we can backtrack to the beginning of the story, with the visit of the fleeing priest to the house of the expatriate American dentist Mr. Tench. Mr. Tench has not had contact with his wife for some two decades, but after the English-speaking priest has visited him, Tench writes a letter to his wife, beginning with the salutation, "Dear Sylvia."

At every point in our reading, we need to keep in mind that the priest is the last priest in his entire province. Other priests have either abandoned their calling, escaped, or been executed. The whiskey priest, hunted like a criminal, never takes the easy way out. As the province becomes his parish, he is the last contact the faithful have with the institutional church. Furthermore, the priest becomes an apologist for the Christian faith in a number of conversations, such as with a woman in the prison room, the mestizo, and preeminently the lieutenant in the closing pages of the novel.

The priest considers himself a failure, and a superficial reading of the story might lead to the same assessment. But once we are alerted to the hidden plot, we can see evidence everywhere of the priest's heroism.

The first American edition of this novel was titled *The Labyrinthine Ways*, an allusion to a line in Francis Thompson's poem "The Hound of Heaven." In Thompson's poem, God pursues and finally conquers a sinner who has spent his lifetime fleeing from him—a tribute to the triumph of divine sovereignty over human waywardness. Like the protagonist in Thompson's poem, the whiskey priest is a latter-day Jonah who does God's work in spite of himself.

For Reflection or Discussion

The religious meaning of the story depends on ferreting out the positive influence of the priest on others. In addition to Mr. Tench and Luis, there are the youthful Coral Fellowes and the lieutenant (forced to confront the religious claims of the priest in an important conversation late in the story), as well as people of the villages through which the priest passes. Where in the story do we see the positive effect the priest has on the lives of others? What evidence is there that the priest has actually been loyal to his clerical calling? What real-life experiences have you had of a minister's influence on you? What has been your experience of an unworthy minister (including yourself) being a positive spiritual influence?

Is Ministry Dependent on a Minister's Worthiness?

This novel highlights two main issues in ministry. One is a minister's failings and unworthiness, including his own awareness of those failings. The priest in this story responds mainly with despair. His specific failings are both personal (such as alcoholism) and professional (such as his ambitiousness early in his career). The novel becomes a mirror for ministers in their own personal and professional failings.

Even more centrally, the story raises the question of the degree to which the life and character of a minister determine the efficacy of the clerical work the minister does. Already back in the fourteenth century, Geoffrey Chaucer portrayed his professional pardoner as a golden-tongued scoundrel (an early day Elmer Gantry) who could move congregants to Christian acts by his preaching despite his own depravity. Graham Greene gives us an even more detailed portrait of the phenomenon in his whiskey priest.

The literary imagination heightens whatever it touches. It paints the issues of life in larger-than-life form so we can see them more clearly. This needs to be factored into our analysis of the question of minister versus ministry as portrayed in *The Power and the Glory*. Greene gives us a super-corrupt priest to highlight the gap between cleric and spiritual calling. Thus heightened, the question is one we cannot avoid considering as we read.

The relevant data has already been covered in the discussion above. We need to reach our own conclusions as we put the two sides of the equation together. On the one side, we have the spectacle of clerical unworthiness—an ever-expanding picture of alcoholism, neglect of professional duties, cowardice, and lack of spirituality. The priest is an archexample of a "clay jar" carrying the gospel.

On the other side, are the characters positively influenced by the priest and the persistence of his faith in the face of persecution. These are offered as evidence that the efficacy of the priest's discharge of some of his duties exists despite the spiritual laxity of the priest's lifestyle. This is where the title of the novel becomes important. The title alludes to the epilogue of the Lord's Prayer, which states, "For thine is the kingdom and the power and the glory forever. Amen." In other words, the survival of the Christian faith in the Mexico of the story is really the triumph of God's power and glory, which are efficacious no matter how corrupt the life of a minister is.

For Reflection or Discussion

Literature is a catalyst to our own thinking about the issues it raises. What have been your experiences of ministerial failing? What have the effects of those failings been? How does the title of this novel serve as an interpretive lens for the question of how a minister's life relates to the spiritual efficacy of his work?

9

The Hammer of God

The Triumph of the Gospel in a Minister's Life

Is not my word like fire, declares the LORD, and like a hammer that breaks the rock in pieces?

Jeremiah 23:29

The Hammer of God was written by a Lutheran pastor and churchman who became a bishop in the Swedish Lutheran Church at the young age of forty-three. To make this appointment even more remarkable, Bo Giertz had been a pastor in small, rural parishes up to that point. The title of the best-known biography of Giertz calls him "an atheist who became a bishop." The publication of *The Hammer of God* in 1941 brought Giertz immediate fame. He wrote the book in a span of six weeks while serving as a rural pastor.

Of all the works covered in this book on pastors in the classics, perhaps no other covers so many issues in ministry as this collection of novellas. The genius of dividing the material into stories of approximately one hundred pages each is that it allows for immense scope. A by-product of the triple-story format is that the continuity across generations gradually dawns on us and reminds us that the bedrock issues of life and ministry are perennial, even though the historical details change. An additional aspect of the book's expansiveness is hinted at in its subtitle: "A Novel about the Cure of Souls." This archaic ecclesiastical phrase means "care of souls," including nurture as well as healing. By the time we end the book, it appears that the souls that have been "cured" include numerous parishioners but also the three ministers.

A common pattern underlies the three stories. Each story starts with the arrival of a young Lutheran pastor against his wish in the same out-of-the-way rural parish. Each pastor begins his ministerial career as a case study in pastoral

Author: Bo Giertz (1905–98)

Nationality: Swedish

Date of first publication: 1941 in Swedish; 1960 in English; 2005 revised English edition with an additional concluding chapter

Approximate number of pages: 325

Available edition: Augsburg

Genres: a trilogy of novellas, Lutheran fiction, Swedish literature

Setting for the story: a small country parish in Sweden; the town where the church is located is called Odesjo; time span of 130 years

Main characters: The format of three novellas results in a crowded cast of characters for the book as a whole. The three main characters are easily identified: they are the protagonists of the successive stories—pastors Savonius, Fridveldt, and Torvik (with the latter generally viewed as a self-portrait of the author). The first two ministers have an important senior minister over them in the parish. Many less-prominent parishioners are instrumental in the spiritual transformations the three protagonists experience.

Plot summary: The overall design of the book is simple: each of the three novellas follows a young Lutheran pastor over approximately a two-year span at the beginning of his ministerial career, all in the same rural parish. The eras covered are, respectively, 1808–10, 1878–80, 1937–40. Each of the three pastors arrives fresh from theological training and decidedly immature (and, in some cases, a nominal rather than true believer). Each of the three attains genuine Christian faith through encounters with (1) parishioners, (2) fellow pastors, and (3) assorted religious movements that were in fact prominent in Sweden during the historical eras covered. There are actually two plotlines in the book: one recounts the "coming of age" spiritual pilgrimages of the three young ministers; the other is an episodic fictional history of a rural Swedish parish.

---

ineptitude. Each is forced to acknowledge his spiritual and ministerial failure, and each undergoes a conversion to mature faith. In addition, all three pastors struggle with the crosswinds of a wide range of Christian movements that the Lutheran author portrays as aberrant; these include at least the following: theological modernism/liberalism; Pentecostalism; pietism; secularism; dead orthodoxy; legalism; revivalism.

While universal in its issues, this is a Lutheran book. Lutheran theologians and church practices form the texture of the book. A pervasive theme is the need to repudiate the claims of law as the heart of the Christian message and instead to embrace the grace of Christ. This motif of law versus grace can of course be traced all the way back to Martin Luther. The eventual resting place at which each of the protagonists arrives at the end of his pilgrimage is Scripture, the atonement of Christ, and the historical Lutheran confessions.

The Lutheran vision of the book is partly encapsulated in a pattern of symbolism that surfaces from time to time and forms the climax of the book. The main symbol appears in the title of the book, which alludes to Jeremiah 23:29: "Is not my word like fire, declares the LORD, and like a hammer that breaks the rock in pieces?" In this trilogy, the sinful human heart is compared to stony ground. The hammer that breaks it is the Word and Spirit of God as they transform people's lives. An additional twist occurs in a sermon that many readers find to be the climax of the book. Here the hill of Golgotha is pictured as a rock of atonement; the human heart is lifted onto this rock and becomes a fertile soil in which the fruits of faith can grow.

"The Hammer of God"

In the first story, Savonius, the young aristocratic graduate of a liberal theological school, arrives at the rural parish that is the setting for all three novellas. The opening scene presents a midwinter party at which the privileged people of the town are settling down to enjoy an evening of cultured socializing. A peasant appears at the door to ask a pastor to attend a dying man twenty-eight miles away. As low man on the totem pole, Savonius is the one who is dispatched on a desperate nighttime journey by horse-drawn carriage. The young pastor goes grudgingly, and when he arrives, he is a spectacle of ineffectualness.

The dying man announces himself to be unregenerate, and yet he knows the Bible and the Lutheran "Church Book" better than the curate. At the last minute, a humble woman appears, conducts a spiritual conversation with the dying man, and leads him to salvation. Savonius goes home knowing that "an altogether new world had opened for him this night. . . . He felt that he had learned more about real godliness in these short morning hours than in all his past life." Savonius gradually reaches a point of conversion (having been earlier stung by the insinuation of the peasant who accompanied him on his carriage ride that he needed to be converted). While the language of "new birth" is not employed, the story makes it clear that Savonius comes to saving faith for the first time in his life (as does Pastor Torvik in the third story).

Once converted, Savonius achieves astounding success as a pastor and preacher. His sermons are so powerful that they draw crowds from neighboring parishes. He surpasses the dean under whom he serves. The church bureaucracy (under the title of "Cathedral Chapter") feels threatened by what is happening and drafts an official statement charging that the curate's "unwise zeal, his fanaticism, and affected manner of preaching had brought about much unrest and confusion."

While under investigation, Savonius continues to conduct the usual round of pastoral duties. He corrects a shoemaker's self-righteous way of dealing with a problem drinker. He encourages the faltering and speaks God's grace to sinners. We thus end the first story in the trilogy pondering the paradoxes of Savonius's ministerial life: he achieves spiritual success from his initial failure but then suffers professional failure by virtue of his spiritual success. But the novella ends on a strongly redemptive note, as Savonius humbly submits to his superiors and confesses his shortcomings as a pastor.

FOR REFLECTION OR DISCUSSION

The opening story in the trilogy evokes reflection on multiple levels, dealing with ordinary Christians in the parish as well as their clergy. How should pastors respond when they discover their own spiritual poverty and inferiority to humble parishioners? What experiences in a church have made you most aware of your deficiencies? How can successful preachers or leaders in a church ministry respond when their very success in the pulpit and parish ministry causes problems? How do ministers cope with official church sanctions against them from a church bureaucracy that may itself be only nominally Christian? More generally, inasmuch as stories achieve their effect by putting before us positive models to emulate and negative models to avoid, what lessons can we learn from the various characters who have played their parts in the story? In all of the questions just noted, it is of course relevant to ponder how the situations that Giertz portrays have occurred in your own life.

"Jesus Only"

As we start to read the second novella, our first impulse might be a slight sense of disorientation, as we need to adjust to a whole new cast of characters. But the process is made easier if we are alert to what carries over. We continue to move in the same parish, approximately seventy years later. Again we follow the adventures (for such they are) of a young minister newly arrived in the parish. Again the young minister is helped along the path by an older clerical mentor, and again we witness a process of struggle and maturation as we vicariously experience a slice of life as a minister encounters it.

The protagonist of the second story is Pastor Fridveldt. He is about as different from Savonius as it is possible to be. He has fallen under the sway of a revivalist movement. In the first major scene of the story, he concludes that his senior in the parish, a rector, is not a true believer because he asks his wife for an alcoholic beverage after dinner in the parsonage. (To render this even more intriguing, the rector's wife shares Fridveldt's disapproval of drinking—even of coffee!) In fact, Fridveldt proceeds to lecture the rector about his need to receive Jesus into his heart.

This young minister does not need conversion but maturing. Upon his arrival, his reputation as a true believer in a church world of nominal Christians creates an immediate sensation. A revival sets in. Of course, there are small setbacks, as when the rector is needed to settle a dispute between two farmers in the church after Fridveldt failed to reconcile them, leaving the young pastor troubled by such sin in a supposedly pietistic or revivalist church.

The young pastor is jolted by a letter from a former university friend who expresses what today we would call a triumphalist view of the Christian life, occasioned by an encounter with Pentecostal fervor that includes as part of its platform a repudiation of infant baptism. Fridveldt becomes convicted that "the lag in the revival might perhaps be due to his own fault or failure." The transforming event in his pastoral life comes when he is distracted from preparing his Transfiguration Day sermon by the need to make a sick call. With his thoughts scattered, he grabs Schartau's *Fifteen Sermons* from his study on his way to the church service and preaches a sermon from the book. The recurrent theme of the sermon is "Jesus only" as the foundation of salvation, a theme that resounded "like hammer blows aimed with unerring precision against the head of a nail." We infer that Fridveldt's response to the sermon is that its power exceeds what he himself might have preached.

A concluding conflict in the novella is the local turmoil about adult baptism. A parish meeting is convened, a debate ensues, and Fridveldt stands strong for the Lutheran tradition of infant baptism (with the element of remaining true to tradition being important in the second story). The concluding note of book 2 is sounded when Fridveldt asks for a cup of coffee after the evening meal at the rector's parsonage. Fridveldt dumbfounds the rector's wife by saying that he has been freed from the curse of the law. The overall progress of Pastor Fridveldt has been from a rigid evangelical to a more compassionate and flexible Christian.

FOR REFLECTION OR DISCUSSION

The second story raises a different set of issues from the first one. What temptations and pitfalls are inherent in a "pietistic" fervor for the Christian life? How can a person take the Christian life seriously without becoming legalistic? What form has this issue taken in your own life or your church's life? What is the role of failure (seen especially in Fridveldt's reading someone else's sermon, which is not, incidentally, carried off in a manner that constitutes plagiarism) in the Christian life? Fridveldt's pastoral life is a seemingly endless succession of demands and distractions from fellow Christians; how does this ring true to your own life? How do you cope with this phenomenon? How does the title of book 2—"Jesus Only"—represent an interpretive framework for the action?

In all three novellas, the chapter titles can be probed for the interpretation they give of the progress of each story; what does this format yield for book 2?

"On This Rock"

Approximately sixty years after the preceding story, young Pastor Torvik arrives in the Odesjo parish. That scenario is now familiar to us as we progress through the book. But book 3 is more rooted in various church movements in Sweden than the first books were. For example, the young pastor arrives fresh from the university, where he had fallen under the sway of the liberal theology that swept through Sweden in Giertz's lifetime. In the book, it is described as "the new theological thinking [that] had accepted the historical [i.e., liberal] view of the Bible, an undogmatic and independent attitude toward the Confessions, and a warm enthusiasm for the church of his fathers" (including an interest in liturgy).

The story opens as Torvik nears the end of his year in the parish. The most brilliant piece of descriptive writing in the book appears early in book 3, with its evocation of a dreary parsonage in the dead of a Swedish winter. As Torvik takes stock of his year in the parish, he tallies up a litany of disappointments. He arrived at a parish in disarray, and things have not improved appreciably. We again follow the local pastor on his routine round of pastoral work, including calls to the ill. Torvik drafts a letter to the Cathedral Chapter requesting a leave of absence.

Then Torvik receives a vision. It is a phantasmagoria of snapshots of parish life, but it is also at some level an encounter with God. Upon awaking, Torvik goes to his study and finds prayer cards with admonitions written on them. These turn out to be the four admonitions of a movement known in real-life Sweden as the legalistic Moral Re-Armament Movement (M.R.A.). Torvik prays for the strength to make a new start and reads his Bible. We read that "it struck him as he read that he had never before read the Bible in this manner; simply to discover how he himself might become a Christian."

The first resolve of his new life is to visit a brother and sister in the parish with the last name of Schenstedt, with whom he had avoided contact. Torvik is self-revealing as he confesses his own lack of true Christianity until this day, and it turns out that the purpose of his visit is to push the Schenstedts on the pathway to faith. Then in a brief, fast-moving scene, (1) a letter arrives from the Cathedral Chapter directing Torvik to remain in the parish as a temporary rector, (2) Gunnar Schenstedt drives up and requests that Torvik visit him and his sister to discuss spiritual matters, and (3) Torvik manages to rush to the post office, retrieve his letter requesting a leave of absence, and tear the letter to shreds.

Just as Torvik is gaining a head of steam, roadblocks appear. On a particularly disastrous day, Torvik receives several critical visitors at the parsonage.

First a woman of the parish registers a list of complaints and accusations. Her basic concern is godly, and her comments have her pastor's best interests at heart, but her message is hard for Torvik to hear: the minister is preaching law but not grace. We also hear for the first time about an organized group of opposition to Torvik.

The woman from the parish happens to visit on the same day as a multi-church Lenten service, so a senior statesman named Pastor Bengtsson has arrived to spend the afternoon at the parsonage before the two of them, and the now-converted Schenstedt (who has become an itinerant evangelist), drive to the town where the service will be held. Pastor Bengtsson challenges Torvik for not teaching the catechism and for not having a sufficiently high view of the Bible; he implies that Torvik still needs to be converted. When Schenstedt arrives to drive them to the church service, he announces that his sister, who had professed Christianity, is in the process of leaving her husband for another man, with the approval of the liberally inclined Schenstedt.

These head-spinning events are a setup for the book's chief triumph. Schenstedt preaches the first sermon at the Lenten service on the liberal theme that "the important thing was not what one believes but what one does." The seasoned Pastor Bengtsson then preaches the sermon that is uniformly praised by those who write about *The Hammer of God*. It is a sermon about "the stone foundation of the heart and the Rock of Atonement on Golgotha." The only means of salvation is to cross from one of these mountains of human destiny to the other on the bridge of God's Word, which "can convict man of sin and lay bare the soul about the Redeemer." Pastor Torvik is so stunned by the power of the sermon that when it is his turn to speak, he simply affirms the truth of the gospel and declares his personal resolve to "be saved in the old way, by grace alone." The minister has taken his critics to heart and is open to spiritual change.

In the car ride back, there is the inevitable and unpleasant disagreement with Schenstedt about his repudiation of such things as the Bible and the historic beliefs of the church, in deference to a vaguely conceived liberalism. Upon returning to the parsonage, Pastor Torvik in effect affirms all that a conservative, traditional Lutheran holds most dear: "Nothing of the old was obsolete: the confession remained just as firm, and the answers the church had given through the centuries were just as conclusive against the many enticements of the modern enthusiasms."

Chapter 9, titled "In the Place of Sinners," presents several difficulties. It did not appear in the first English translation of the book, perhaps because it is long, somewhat desultory, and arguably blunts the force of what has preceded. On the other hand, it gives symmetry to the book as a whole, completing the third set of three chapters. It also brings the novel full circle: at the end of the last novella, as at the beginning of the first novella, Russia threatens Sweden with war.

It is in this final chapter that the minister's wife truly shines. Britta gives her husband a salutary caution and takes the initiative to adopt the son of Torvik's rival. At the very end of the book, when he receives news of Schenstedt's final repentance and sure salvation, Torvik rushes to share the news with Britta as his partner in ministry.

For Reflection or Discussion

Part of the genius of The Hammer of God *is the way in which the book captures the reality of a day in the life of a pastor or church member. With what aspects of the life of a minister or church member do you most strongly resonate as you read book 3? All three stories recount a turning point in the life of a pastor; what have been the breakthrough experiences in your life and ministry? Pastor Torvik is simultaneously bedeviled and spiritually improved by people who criticize him; what examples do you find, and what carryovers to real life occur to you? Torvik finds it necessary to resist certain modern religious movements and viewpoints that swirl around him; what bridges can you build between Torvik's world and yours? What religious movements have you found most helpful or most dangerous (and therefore needing to be countered)? The last two paragraphs of chapter 8 ("A Heart of Stone and a Rock of Salvation") are the moment of epiphany toward which the whole book moves; what are the important elements in this Christian credo? Torvik affirms historic Lutheranism, based ultimately on the Bible; in terms of theological and church orientation, what is the bedrock on which you have built your lasting refuge? In keeping with Torvik's partnership with Britta, as portrayed in chapter 9, what are the most important lessons you have learned about sharing the joys and trials of ministry as a married couple?*

10

Cry, the Beloved Country

Sanctified for Service through Suffering

There is no fear in love, but perfect love casts out fear.

1 John 4:18

Cry, the Beloved Country is widely regarded as the definitive novel of the South African experience. Although the book was written more than half a century ago and published even before apartheid was established as a system of racial segregation, its hopeful yet honest treatment of social issues has ongoing relevance for South Africa and the world. Alan Paton invited his readers to embrace this perspective when he described his novel as "a song of love for one's far distant country . . . the land where you were born."

To read *Cry, the Beloved Country* is to become immersed in the tragic complexities of racial conflict that gripped South Africa in the 1940s and afterward. Paton vividly evokes the events of that time and place: the political speeches, the rise of the black shanty towns, the mining and transportation strikes, the personal sacrifices that blacks and whites both made to serve one another across racial lines. He also addresses some of the hardest challenges that remain for South Africa, such as the corruption of power, the ever-present danger of criminal violence, and the need for new social structures to rebuild broken families in divided communities.

All of this forms the setting for the dramatic story of loss and forgiveness that Paton tells about one man—a minister—who endures painful suffering in a fallen world and struggles to understand the purposes of God for his life, his family, his church, and his community. By the grace of God and through the ministry of his people, that man perseveres in faith, hope, and love. His story gives hope to the world by showing what one godly person can do in response to its heartbreaking need for justice and mercy.

Author: Alan Paton (1903–88)

Nationality: South African

Date of first publication: 1948

Approximate number of pages: 300

Available edition: Scribner

Genres: novel, quest story, pilgrimage story, murder story, regional writing, historical fiction, nature writing

Setting for the story: South Africa in the 1940s, shortly before the imposition of the system of racial separation known as apartheid; more specifically, the rural valley of the Umzimkulu and the troubled city of Johannesburg

Main characters: The central figures are the Rev. Stephen Kumalo, an old Anglican priest in the rural Zulu parish of Ndotsheni, and James Jarvis, the wealthy English landowner whose farm overlooks the valley where Kumalo's congregation lives, works, and worships. Other members of the Kumalo and Jarvis families play significant roles, especially their wives and their only sons (Absalom Kumalo and Arthur Jarvis). Kumalo's guide in Johannesburg is a fellow priest who becomes his "friend of friends," the Rev. Theophilus Msimangu. The land of South Africa also has such a strong presence in the novel that it virtually stands as a character in its own right.

Plot summary: *Cry, the Beloved Country* is divided into three parts (roughly 150, 100, and 50 pages, respectively). The novel opens with Kumalo leaving on a quest to find and rescue his wayward sister and prodigal son from the dangers of Johannesburg, where the disintegration of South African society is mirrored by the downfall of the priest's own family. Part 1 ends with a crisis of faith, as Kumalo's worst fear is realized: his son, Absalom, is in prison for the murder of Arthur Jarvis, a young white activist for black civil rights. Part 2 begins with a second journey, as James Jarvis travels to Johannesburg to grieve his son's death and, in doing so, to confront his prejudice against black South Africans. When Absalom is convicted of murder and sentenced to death, Kumalo prepares to return home, but not before an unexpected encounter with Jarvis gives him the opportunity to seek forgiveness for his son's crime. Despite the great loss that Kumalo and Jarvis have each suffered, their homecoming in part 3 is a story of healing and redemption, with restored and renewed relationships in the family and the community, including Kumalo's church.

The Tribe Is Broken

The sufferings of Stephen Kumalo begin when he goes to Johannesburg to help his sister. The city is an archetypal den of iniquity, and the old priest's journey there unexpectedly exposes him to the full range of human depravity.

Virtually the first thing that happens to Kumalo in Johannesburg is that a man takes advantage of him at the bus station, stealing a one pound note. This incident shows how out of place and vulnerable Kumalo is in the big city, but it also serves as a portent of all the troubles he is about to face. The city is a dangerous place that uses and abuses its victims.

In Johannesburg, Kumalo witnesses the sin of fallen humanity at its widest level, in the structures of human society. He sees it in the racial prejudice of white South Africans, of course, but also in the rising violence of the black community. Whatever individual misconduct Kumalo witnesses—and whatever wrongdoing he reads about in the newspaper—has a communal context: "The house that is broken, and the man that falls apart when the house is broken, these are the tragic things. That is why children break the law, and old white people are robbed and beaten."

As Kumalo sees the sins of the city, he laments the breakdown of South African society: "The tribe was broken," he finally admitted to himself, "and would be mended no more." Yet what causes him the greatest distress is the destruction this brings to his own family.

He sees this breakdown first in his sister Gertrude, whose sickness is not physical, as he had expected, but spiritual. Even before Kumalo enters her home, her moral decline is signaled by the loud and careless laughter of her companions. Upon entering, he quickly discovers that her sinful lifestyle of prostitution and alcohol abuse prevents her from taking proper care of her son. By her own admission, she has become a bad woman.

As Kumalo continues the quest to locate his long-lost son, he has a growing fear that he, too, has fallen into sin. People who know Absalom report that he has fallen in with a bad crowd. The pastor's son is lost in the city, in more ways than one. Eventually Kumalo learns that his son had been living with a young girl and that together they have a child. He begins to ask the agonizing questions of all parents who grieve for a prodigal child: "Where had they failed? What had they done, or left undone, that their son had become a thief, moving like a vagabond from place to place, living with a girl who was herself no more than a child, father of a child who would have had no name?"

Kumalo hopes against hope that his anxious concern for his son is unjustified, but in the end his darkest fear is realized. The iniquity of Johannesburg has had its disastrous effect on a simple boy from the country, and the wayward son is guilty of murder. Even the city's best efforts at redemption (the work of the reform school) have failed in Absalom's case, a detail from the novel that reflects the author's own experience as the superintendent of a reformatory for four hundred black youths.

The overwhelming suffering that Kumalo endures is so disheartening that it leads to a crisis of faith. As a priest, he is ashamed that his own sister has become a notorious woman. As a father, he is brokenhearted that he cannot touch his son's heart, helping him to see beyond his self-pity far enough to repent of the evil he has done. Thus, Kumalo is afflicted by a particular kind of suffering—the suffering that is caused by the sins of people he describes as living "without faith or purpose."

FOR REFLECTION OR DISCUSSION

Cry, the Beloved Country *explores both the personal and the communal effects of sin. Where does the sin of your community bring the most suffering to your soul? What threats do the prevailing sins of the surrounding culture pose to the spiritual well-being of your family? In what ways does Kumalo's journey to Johannesburg remind you of your own experiences in life and ministry?*

A Selfish and Sinful Man

Kumalo endures the sufferings of a sinful world with noble dignity. His piety, generosity, and Christian morality stand in contrast to the conduct of his wayward family members and to the harsh spiritual climate of a fallen city. Indeed, Kumalo's character and conduct are nearly heroic.

The list of the priest's virtues is lengthy. Kumalo has a warm, affectionate, and playful relationship with the various children he meets throughout the novel. He treats others with kindness, in the full biblical sense of the word. This is evident in nearly all his interactions, but especially in his commitment to receive Absalom's girlfriend and her unborn child as his own daughter and grandson. He is quick to forgive others and to have compassion on those who have fallen into sin, like his sister Gertrude. Kumalo is also deeply dedicated to the duties and sacrifices of his calling as a servant of the gospel: to public and private prayer, to reading God's Word, and to giving up worldly gain for service in the church. The priest's humility, gentleness, and faithfulness are evident to everyone. He is "so good," Mrs. Lithebe says to Gertrude, "that there is no word for it."

Yet for all his virtues, Stephen Kumalo has his own sins to confess, and thus the sanctification of his soul is central to the development of the novel. Although Kumalo's godly character stands in marked contrast to the misdeeds of his family and the evils of the surrounding society, his own spiritual failures threaten to hinder him from doing the full work of mercy and justice that God has for him to do in his parish. The words Rev. Theophilus Msimangu applies to himself also apply to Kumalo: "I am not kind. I am a selfish and sinful man, but God put his hands on me, that is all."

Kumalo's misdeeds may seem smaller than the crimes of others, yet they betray a selfish and sinful heart. On the train to Johannesburg, he boasts to other passengers that he often travels to the city on business—a lie of self-aggrandizement. Later, the priest also lies to his brother, trying to convince him that there is a political informant among his friends at the barber shop—a lie told to injure his brother. This is not the first time Kumalo has succumbed to the temptation to hurt someone. He does the same thing in his bitter words to his wife and in his angry confrontation with Absalom's girlfriend, when he bitterly attacks her character and virtually threatens her with sexual violence.

There are times when Kumalo's angry words hurt both himself and others, including the people he loves. But his greatest temptation is the sin of despair, of abandoning his hope and faith in the goodness of God. The word *fear* is often used to describe the state of the priest's soul. His fears begin when he first receives a letter from Johannesburg and wonders whether it might concern the fate of his son. Kumalo does not know where Absalom is, what he is doing, or why he never writes home. His fears grow as he reaches the city and sees more of its vice. Then comes the news that a white man was shot by a black man in a burglary, and Kumalo fears the worst. "This thing," he says. "This thing. Here in my heart there is nothing but fear. Fear, fear, fear." Later Kumalo describes this fear as "something too great to be borne." Even God seems to have gone against him, and for a time he is unable to believe that God is at work; there is "nothing in the world but fear and pain."

How does Kumalo overcome these fears? Partly through prayer. As his fears mount, he makes the words of Psalm 23 a confession of his faith: "I shall fear no evil, if Thou art with me." "*Tixo*," he later prays, using one of the African names for God, "forsake me not." These prayers are answered in part through the ministry of the gospel. As Kumalo hears his friend Msimangu read the Bible and preach to the blind people of Ezenzeleni, he recovers his faith.

Kumalo addresses other sins through the hard spiritual work of confessing them both to God and to his neighbor. On his first visit to prison, after Absalom has been arrested, the priest upbraids his son for not fighting against the devil. "Oh boy," he says, "can you not say you fought the devil? Can you not say that you wept for your sins, and vowed to make amends, and stood upright, and stumbled, and fell again? Why did you not struggle against him?"

Here the priest speaks to his son from his own experience of struggling with the devil, of weeping for his sins and standing up again. Every time Kumalo hurts someone, he offers personal repentance—to his wife, to Absalom's girlfriend, to Jarvis, to his brother. He also confesses his sins to God, especially at the end of the novel when he goes up the mountain and recounts his sins, remembering them "as well as he could" and repenting of them "as fully as he could," praying for absolution.

By the grace of God, fruitful ministry grows from a heart that is gaining ground against sin. Stephen Kumalo struggled with anger and ambition. What are some of the ways these sins commonly tempt people in ministry? Kumalo's besetting sin was fear. What fears tempt you to despair? What other sins are most likely to hinder your fruitfulness in ministry? How are you fighting against them?

The Love That Casts Out Fear

As he faces the struggles of life, family, and ministry in a fallen world, Kumalo is not alone. He is deeply blessed by the love and care of people in the Christian community. Only love has the power to transform, and their perfect love casts out his fear.

Some of the loving care Kumalo receives is practical, such as the help of the head of the reformatory in finding his son, or the benevolence of Mr. Carmichael, the lawyer who takes Absalom's case "for God," not for money. Then there is Mrs. Lithebe, the church member in Johannesburg who graciously welcomes the priest into her own home, together with his sister, his nephew, and eventually Absalom's girlfriend. And there is also James Jarvis, who in part 3 of the novel does so much to save the dying children of Ndotsheni, to improve agricultural methods, and to rebuild the village church.

The care that Kumalo receives from the Christian community is also spiritual—the cure of his soul. For example, although Father Vincent struggles to find the right words for Kumalo, his spiritual guidance is sound: he should rest and pray, with thanksgiving, and especially for the needs of others.

Kumalo receives more complete spiritual counsel from Msimangu, the young priest who first summons him to Johannesburg. In addition to serving as his faithful guide in the quest to find his son, Msimangu becomes Kumalo's spiritual confidante. The young priest prays for his older colleague and often exhorts him to take courage, not to give up hope until the boy is found. When necessary, Msimangu even rebukes Kumalo for his ungodly fear: "I say it is time to turn. This is madness, that is bad enough. But it is also sin, which is worse. I speak to you as a priest." Kumalo's willingness to receive these words as a kindness is a clear indication of his humility before God, while Msimangu's courage to offer them is the proof of his love. The young priest helps most of all by his ministry of the Bible—the "book of golden words." His sermon to the blind is intended as much for Kumalo as for anyone, and in the end it is the Word of God that brings the protagonist to full spiritual recovery.

Upon his return to the valley of the Umzimkulu, the old priest is deeply blessed by the loving welcome of his people. With the news of his return, the children come running and shouting down the hills in the darkness. The entire congregation gathers outside the church, where they greet their shepherd's return with songs of thanksgiving. Kumalo goes inside to pray with his people, and he finds the courage to ask for his sister and his son to be forgiven their trespasses—a prayer that indirectly yet publicly acknowledges his own weakness. Instantly he recognizes that the courage to offer this prayer has not come from his own soul but from the love of his people. As it turns out, they already know what he has suffered in Johannesburg, but rather than rejecting him, as he feared, they accept him with healing love. In the joy of his return, Kumalo's pain is forgotten.

FOR REFLECTION OR DISCUSSION

Kumalo's experiences raise important issues for spiritual care in the church. In what practical and spiritual ways has your own ministry been helped by the loving care of the people of God? Recall one or two of the most constructive rebukes you have received. What did you learn about the right way to confront someone's sin? For people in spiritual leadership, the disclosure of family troubles requires mature judgment. What principles have you found helpful in handling such situations in the church or in other ministry contexts?

The House and the Soul Restored

Back in Johannesburg, when he visited Msimangu's mission to the blind, Kumalo was momentarily "caught up in a vision, as man so often is when he sits in a place of ashes and destruction." His vision was to return to the valley of the Umzimkulu to repair, rebuild, and restore the tribe that had been broken. What the priest saw in the city and suffered in his family overwhelmed him with painful sorrow. But on the basis of these experiences he saw that "one could go back knowing better the things that one fought against, knowing better the kind of thing that one must build."

In order to do the sacred work of rebuilding a community, Kumalo's own soul had to be restored to faith, with hope and love. When he first returns to his church, a friend asks if he still trusts in God. In a world full of trouble and destruction, does the priest still believe? "I believe," Kumalo says, affirming his faith. "I have learned that kindness and love can pay for pain and suffering—so in my suffering I can believe."

In his suffering, Kumalo can also serve. He can do what Father Vincent described as the work of "Christ in us, crying that men may be succored and forgiven, even when He Himself is forsaken." Earlier Kumalo had wanted to tell his brother that "the man who fights for justice must be cleansed and purified." By the end of the novel, these words prove to be prophetic of his own sanctification. Kumalo's sufferings have not made him weak but stronger in the service of God. Chastened by the sins of his family, humbled through his own repentance, and finally healed by Christian love, Kumalo is ready to work for the salvation of his people.

Even when he is depressed by doubts about ever seeing his vision accomplished, Kumalo continues to depend on the power of God. Sitting alone in the church, he asks, "Where was the great vision that he had seen at Ezenzeleni, the vision born of such great suffering? Of how a priest could make of his parish a real place of life for his people, and preparation for his children? Was he old then and finished? Or was his vision a delusion, and these things beyond all helping? No power but the power of God could bring about such a miracle, and he prayed again briefly, 'Into Thy hands, oh God, I commend Ndotsheni.'"

In the closing pages of the novel, Kumalo's prayers are answered. After months of drought, the rains begin to fall, healing the sickness of the land. Kumalo is fully reconciled to Jarvis, who pours his money and energy into helping the black community. Jarvis gives Kumalo milk to save the lives of dying children. He hires a teacher to train people in the proper techniques of agriculture. He begins building a dam to control the water supply. At the very end he promises to build Kumalo a new church, which will stand as a symbol of spiritual renewal. There is new life in the valley—"an intimation of the divine."

There may even be hope for the salvation of Absalom, and for Africa, the beloved country. When Kumalo goes up the mountain, his last prayers are for his son, offered on the day of his execution. "My son, my son, my son," he cries, praying to the "Christ of the abundant mercy." And as Kumalo looks to the east, he sees the first light of dawn, bringing the hope of a brighter day.

For Reflection or Discussion

Stephen Kumalo is sanctified for service through his suffering. In what ways have the sufferings of life and family helped to prepare you for ministry? What important life experiences have given you a vision for the kingdom work God has called you to do? What are your prayers for the restoration of your community, and how are you seeing God answer them?

11

Silence

Becoming like Jesus in His Death

We are . . . persecuted, but not forsaken . . . always carrying in the body the
death of Jesus, so that the life of Jesus may also be manifested in our bodies.

2 Corinthians 4:8–10

While visiting a Tokyo museum, the novelist Shusaku Endo saw a *fumie*—an iconographic image of Jesus Christ in bronze and wood. The *fumie* was blackened by the feet of seventeenth-century apostates who chose to trample the face of the crucified Christ rather than suffer torture and death at the hands of their overlords.

Seeing the *fumie* raised questions for Endo about Japanese Christianity, about the incarnation and crucifixion of the Son of God, and about his own faith in Christ. What was ministry like for the priests who tried to serve God in those days of persecution and apostasy? Endo wondered if he would have had the courage to suffer torture or would have trampled Jesus underfoot. *Silence* emerged from these questions, and also from Endo's lifelong quest to reconcile his Japanese upbringing with the claims of a gospel he first heard in Europe.

Knowing some historical background is crucial to understanding the novel. Christianity began in Japan around 1549 through the pioneering work of the Society of Jesus. By the end of the sixteenth century, there were hundreds of thousands of Japanese Christians—so many that Francis Xavier famously described Japan as "the country in the Orient most suited to Christianity."

The first portent of persecution was a 1587 edict banning foreign missionaries. Though this attempt to stem the tide of Christianity failed, the following decades saw growing persecution of the church. Twenty-six missionaries were crucified in 1597 near Nagasaki, where Endo's novel is set. Then, in 1614, the

Author: Shusaku Endo (1923–96)

Nationality: Japanese

Date of first publication: 1966 as *Chinmoku*; translated into English in 1969

Approximate number of pages: 200

Available edition: Taplinger Publishing Company

Genres: novel, historical fiction, passion play in prose form, journey story, regional writing, nature writing

Setting for the story: islands and villages near Nagasaki (and the city itself) in the late 1630s, when samurai were compelling Christians either to apostatize by trampling a holy image of Christ (an icon called the *fumie*) or else be tortured and killed

Main characters: Father Sebastian Rodrigues, the Portuguese priest and missionary to Japan whose spiritual struggles and temptation to deny Christ form the central drama of the novel; his mentor, Father Christovao Ferreira, who is rumored to have apostatized; Kichijiro, the Judas figure who shadows Rodrigues throughout the book as both his betrayer and his parishioner; Inoue, the malevolent magistrate who captures Rodrigues and threatens him with torture if he will not trample the face of Christ

Plot summary: The book opens with the unthinkable news that after more than thirty years of missionary work in Japan, the inspirational Jesuit priest Christovao Ferreira has succumbed to the tortures of "the pit" and apostatized. In disbelief, his protégé Sebastian Rodrigues smuggles himself into Japan to search for the truth. The first half of the novel consists of letters from Father Rodrigues to his superiors in Europe—letters in which he describes the sufferings of the underground church and his own feeble efforts to minister in the face of persecution. Eventually the priest is captured by Inoue's soldiers, and from then on the story is narrated in the third person. As Rodrigues strains to hear the voice of God and struggles with his painful dilemma—whether to suffer torture or deny Christ—he comes face-to-face with Ferreira, who cleverly tempts his former student to join in his apostasy. The novel's climax comes when Rodrigues prepares to trample the *fumie* . . . and meets Christ in a surprising way.

Tokagawa shogunate ordered the immediate expulsion of all foreign missionaries, forcing the church underground.

The decade of most intense persecution was the 1630s, when there were wide-scale massacres of Christians who refused to deny their faith. The conventional ritual for apostasy was to step on a *fumie*, one of the bronze icons Japanese believers used to remind them of Christ and his cross. Many believers resisted the temptation to renounce their faith in this way, choosing instead to be burned, scalded, or crucified. Perhaps the most brutal torture was the *ana-tsurushi*, in which victims were hung upside down in a pit of filthy excrement and then cut on the head so they would slowly bleed to death.

The men who faced the most intense pressure to apostatize were the priests who remained in Japan to maintain a secret ministry of Word and sacrament. The enemies of the church believed that the best way to break the will of ordinary believers was to compel their leaders to deny Jesus Christ. Their first and most famous apostate was the head of the Jesuit mission, Father Christovao Ferreira, who could not endure the agonies of "the pit" and chose instead to trample the *fumie*.

These events establish the context for *Silence* (in which both Ferreira and his tormentor appear as major characters) and set the stage for Father Rodrigues in his desperate attempt to remain faithful to Christ in ministry.

"Trample! Trample!"

The story of Father Rodrigues is told in a direct, spare, linear narrative that belies its underlying complexity. On the surface, the priest's defining choice is whether he will have the courage to suffer torture or will apostatize. Will he defend Christ or defile his holy image?

From the outset, Rodrigues is fully aware of the danger in traveling to Japan. Yet he is full of zeal to atone for Ferreira's apostasy, which he regards as a defeat for the Christian faith. His goal in ministry is to serve the church and vindicate the gospel by remaining faithful unto death. Thus, he is determined not to apostatize like Kichijiro, in his cringing cowardice, or like Ferreira himself, whom Rodrigues says "groveled like a dog before the infidels and cast away everything to which he had hitherto devoted his life."

Once the priest arrives in Japan, local Christians quickly take him to a hut in the mountains, where he can escape detection by the local authorities. But as he witnesses the sufferings of the Japanese church and engages in his priestly duties, he has a growing willingness to expose himself to possible capture. Rodrigues refuses to let undue caution get in the way of ministry. So he opens the door to strangers from another village and hears their confession of sin, even though he cannot be certain they will not betray him.

As he takes more risks, Rodrigues has a growing awareness that getting captured and being tempted to apostatize will be his destiny. He often wonders how he will respond when he finally has to make his fateful choice. Is he ready to face torture and death for the cause of Christ, or will he run away like Kichijiro?

Rodrigues fears that he might well trample the *fumie*—a fear that only grows when he is put in prison and sees firsthand how persecution robs some believers of their faith. A foreshadowing of his choice comes when Mokishi, Ichizo, and Kichijiro face the *fumie*. The three men ask their priest what they should do when they are ordered to step on the image of Christ. Rodrigues knows that the believer's true calling is to stand firm like Father Gabriel, who said, "I had rather this foot were cut off than that I should trample on this image." But without thinking, Rodrigues cries out "Trample! Trample!" Immediately he knows he has said the wrong thing, but he has said it for a worthy reason: to spare his brothers the pains of persecution. Later he will say something similar to a fellow priest: "Apostatize! You must apostatize!"

For his own part, Father Rodrigues has sworn that he will never apostatize. But in the end, the *fumie* confronts him with an unexpected dilemma. During the awful night before his ordeal, the priest hears the anguished moans of tortured believers. The next morning Ferreira tells Rodrigues that unless he apostatizes, his friends will be suspended in "the pit." The priest had expected to choose between honoring Christ and sparing himself the pains of persecution. As it turns out, however, his real choice is between obedience and love: will he do his duty not to deny Christ, or will he show mercy to Japanese believers by saving them from persecution?

Rodrigues chooses to apostatize. The cock that crows immediately afterward indicates that he has denied Christ. The priest knows his betrayal cannot be justified. And yet, paradoxically, his choice was not made out of weakness and fear but out of pity and mercy—an apostasy of love.

For Reflection or Discussion

Most Christians never face a life-or-death dilemma like the one Father Rodrigues faced. Yet we are all tempted to avoid some of the hardships that come with the call to serve in ministry, or even to deny Christ in some way. When do you find it hardest to be faithful to Christ? In what ways are you tempted to act out of self-preservation rather than making costly choices to serve God and love other people?

"Feed My Lambs"

As Rodrigues journeys toward Nagasaki, where he will make his defining choice, his soul is on a similar pilgrimage. His goal is not to become a martyr but to serve as a good shepherd. In pursuing this goal, he comes to a deeper understanding of his calling to feed God's flock.

The desire to serve as a faithful shepherd was in the priest's heart from the beginning. He wanted to fulfill his duty to the Japanese church. "In that stricken land," he said, "the Christians have lost their priests and are like a flock of sheep without a shepherd. Someone must go to give them courage and to ensure that the tiny flame of faith does not die out."

The priest's first ministry is to the people of Tomogi. In his secret hut, Rodrigues teaches them how to pray, hears the confession of their sins, and offers them the sacrament of the Mass. Never before has he felt so deeply how meaningful it is to live the life of a priest. Yet his thoughts often turn to all the villages that are still without a priest. Rodrigues wants to "seek out and find the lonely and abandoned flock." But he finds his true place of ministry after he is captured, when he blesses and teaches his fellow prisoners, hears the confession of their sins, encourages them with words of biblical comfort, and offers for them the first "real prayer" he has ever prayed.

In serving as a shepherd for lost and lonely sheep, Father Rodrigues is following the example of the Good Shepherd. This connection is made explicit when he says that in preaching the gospel he is drawn to the beautiful face of Jesus Christ. Rodrigues explains that his vision of that face (which appears more than one hundred times in the novel) is shaped by the icons of the early church, which customarily presented Christ in the form of a shepherd. This is the Christ that every minister is called to serve: the Shepherd who said, "Feed my lambs."

"The good shepherd lays down his life for the sheep" (John 10:11), and Rodrigues follows Christ in this respect as well. *Silence* contains dozens of biblical allusions that explicitly connect the priest's life to the passion of Christ, from Gethsemane to Calvary. To cite one obvious example, Rodrigues is betrayed for pieces of silver thrown at the feet of Kichijiro, who plays Judas to the priest's Jesus. Even small details help connect Rodrigues to the life of Christ, such as when the priest sucks sea water from his fingers and is reminded of the vinegar Jesus was offered on the cross (Matt. 27:48), or when the horse he rides into Nagasaki is described as looking like a donkey, such as the one Jesus rode into Jerusalem (John 12:14–15). Allusions to incidents surrounding the trial, torture, and crucifixion of Jesus Christ are so pervasive that *Silence* is virtually a passion play in prose form.

Rodrigues shares in the sufferings of Christ, becoming like him in his death (see Phil. 3:10). While he is still on the island of Hirado, the priest catches a glimpse of his own face in a pool—"a tired, hollow face" that reminds him of a crucified man. Similarly, the *fumie* he sees at the end of the novel is ugly and emaciated, hinting that through his sufferings, his face has become the face of Christ.

The priest's closest connection to Christ comes at the moment of his apostasy, when he makes the choice Jesus made: to be damned so that others might be saved (cf. Rom. 9:3). Rodrigues does not wish to step on the *fumie*. Indeed, he knows that to deny Christ is to fall under God's condemnation. Yet because of his pity for those who suffer and his desire to deliver them, Rodrigues is willing to suffer this loss: "The priest becomes Christ by surrendering Christ, which is what Christ did." Paradoxically, then, his greatest humiliation turns out to be the moment when he is drawn closest to Christ and shares most in his sufferings.

Father Rodrigues grows in his understanding of his calling as a priest. What life experiences have shaped your understanding of your own calling (whether as a pastor or to some other form of ministry)? What details in the novel allude to Christ and his passion? At what times in your own life or ministry do you feel drawn most closely to Christ in his sufferings?

The Silence of God

Although *Silence* is not the title Endo chose for his novel, it does introduce an important theme. As Father Rodrigues suffers and prays for his fellow sufferers in the persecuted church, God seems strangely silent.

Rodrigues makes his missionary journey "for the conversion of Japan and the glory of God." In keeping with these lofty goals, his first letters home are brimming with spiritual confidence in the power and grace of God. Yet the sufferings of the church and the hardships of ministry raise difficult questions: "Why has Our Lord imposed this torture and this persecution on poor Japanese peasants?" "Why have you abandoned us so completely?" Despite the priest's best efforts to justify the ways of God, his questions go unanswered. So do his prayers: "Already twenty years have passed since the persecution broke out; the black soil of Japan has been filled with the lament of so many Christians; the red blood of priests has flowed profusely; the walls of the churches have fallen down; and in the face of this terrible and merciless sacrifice offered up to Him, God has remained silent."

The silence grows deafening when Mokichi and Ichizo are fastened to their crosses and left to drown in the rising tide. At first Rodrigues hears their triumphant song: "We're on our way to the temple of Paradise." But soon there is only an unfathomable silence. Later, when Ferreira tempts him to apostatize, Rodrigues pleads for God to speak: "Lord, it is now that you should break the silence." God does not break the silence then, however, but only when the priest apostatizes. As he raises his foot to tread on the *fumie*, Christ speaks from the image with an audible voice: "Trample! Trample! I more than anyone know of the pain in your foot. Trample! It was to be trampled on by men that I was born into this world. It was to share men's pain that I carried my cross."

"Trample!" is not a command, as the English translation would seem to indicate; as several scholars have noted, the Japanese verb is permissive rather than imperative. "You may trample me," Christ is saying. So God speaks a word of grace to the priest's anguished soul. Treading on the *fumie* is a blameworthy apostasy, which will cause him to be rejected by the church. Yet Christ does not condemn. Rather, he identifies with Rodrigues in the suffering of his Christlike sacrifice, permitting him to apostatize out of pity for other victims of "the pit."

The God of *Silence* is not silent, therefore, but a God who speaks. This is confirmed by the protagonist's closing lines, in which Father Rodrigues confesses his faith: "Our Lord was not silent. Even if he had been silent, my life until this day would have spoken of him."

FOR REFLECTION OR DISCUSSION

When has God seemed silent to you, and how has he spoken to you out of or after the silence? What are the best ways to minister to someone who is suffering the silence of God? What is helpful to say or not to say?

The Swamp of Japan

An underlying conflict between East and West runs through *Silence*, as it ran through the author's own life. Although Endo identified himself as a Christian, he had a lifelong struggle to make Western Christianity fit into his fundamentally Japanese (that is to say, Buddhist) perspective. When he was baptized at age thirteen, his Roman Catholic mother compelled him to wear a ready-made but ill-fitting Western suit. Endo often remarked that he had been trying ever since to fashion his Christian faith into "a Japanese garment that would fit my Japanese body."

We see a similar conflict in the ministry of Father Rodrigues. In his early letters, Rodrigues expresses admiration for Francis Xavier and the golden age of the Jesuit mission to Japan. "The great missionaries," he calls them—men who sailed around the world to preach the gospel: "What sweat and toil it had taken to plunge the spade into this barren soil, then to fertilize it, to cultivate it until it reached this present stage. Yes, the seed had been sown; it sprouted forth with vigor."

Later Rodrigues will come to view the triumphs of past missionaries with a sense of ironic distance, but he could still see the fruit of their work in the lives of the peasants he served. Even in the years when they worshiped without a priest, brave lay leaders had organized the people for teaching, prayer, and baptism. Yet the priest soon begins to doubt whether the Japanese church has much of a future, especially after seeing all the churches that the shoguns have destroyed. Perhaps Christianity is a European tree that cannot be transplanted onto Asian soil.

Father Rodrigues also begins to doubt the effectiveness of his own ministry, which formerly he had regarded as crucial to the survival of the church. "If you die," says a voice inside, "the Japanese church dies with you." Yet the priest comes to believe that his ministry has only brought greater hardship.

Rodrigues had come to lay down his life for the Japanese, but they are laying down their lives for him, "the foreigner who has brought disaster to them all."

Are the sufferings of Japanese Christians a sign that Christianity will always be a foreign imposition? The church's detractors say that the "great missionaries" had nothing but contempt for Japanese culture. Even Rodrigues, who has done everything he can to identify with the Japanese, admits that Japan is "a people and a country which you can never understand." According to Inoue—the man who orchestrates the priest's apostasy—cultural ignorance has been his downfall: "Father, you were not defeated by me. You were defeated by this swamp of Japan."

Shusaku Endo has prepared us for the image of the swamp by describing Japan as a place of heavy rain and oppressive heat, full of buzzing insects and noisy birds. But he does not believe Japan is inhospitable to the gospel. On the contrary, Father Rodrigues shows how the sufferings of a humiliated Christ can touch the Japanese soul.

In telling the story of the mission to Japan, *Silence* moves from a triumphant church to a suffering church. Rodrigues makes a similar journey in his own relationship to Christ, moving from a theology of glory to a theology of the cross. There is a transformation in the priest's image of Christ. Early in the novel, he sees a face full of vigor and strength—an exalted Christ. The face he later sees in the *fumie* is "sunken and utterly exhausted"—a crucified and humiliated Christ. Yet this is the authentic Jesus that Japan needs, that we all need: a rejected Christ who suffered for us and knows our weakness. Such a Christ is an embarrassment to every culture, but he is also our only hope.

FOR REFLECTION OR DISCUSSION

Silence raises important questions about contextualizing the gospel—not just in Japan, or merely for missionaries, but anyplace where Christianity confronts culture. What idolatries make your own culture inhospitable to the gospel? Due to lack of cultural awareness, what mistakes have you or your church made in sharing the gospel? What aspects of the person and work of Christ make the strongest connection with the spiritual longings of your culture?

12

Gilead

Finishing Well

I have fought the good fight, I have finished the race, I have kept the faith.

2 Timothy 4:7

Marilynne Robinson's Pulitzer Prize–winning novel *Gilead* is a richly textured exploration of family life and pastoral ministry in small-town America. *Gilead* is partly the story of a November/May romance between an aging minister and a much younger woman who wanders into his church and then into his heart. It is also the story of a father's love for his only son, who is still too young to understand everything he needs to know about life. Then, too, it is a story about what it is like to grow old and die, leaving one's family behind for the glory beyond.

At a broader level, Robinson's book can also be read as an imaginative retelling of the history of Protestant Christianity in the United States, with members of the Ames family standing in for major traditions and character types of American religion after the Puritans. The blazing, one-eyed, gun-toting abolitionist John Ames is a visionary prophet in the tradition of John Brown, preaching the sons of his church off to fight for the Union, and then after the Civil War proclaiming the righteous purity of their sacrifice. His namesake becomes a pacifist, claiming that fighting such wars has "*nothing to do with Jesus. Nothing.*"

The oldest son of the next generation is named "Edwards," after America's greatest theologian (Jonathan Edwards). But he drops the *s* in college, a small but telling indication that he is moving further away from Puritan theology. Edward goes to study theology in Gottingen, where he falls under the sway

Author: Marilynne Robinson (1943–)

Nationality: American

Date of first publication: 2004 (the companion novel, *Home*, was published in 2008)

Approximate number of pages: 250

Available edition: Farrar, Straus and Giroux

Genres: fictional autobiography, epistolary novel, small-town fiction, farewell address, fatherly instruction

Setting for the story: Gilead, Iowa, in the summer of 1956; most of the action occurs in the manse of the town's Congregational church

Main characters: John Ames, a third-generation Congregationalist minister who has stayed in his hometown for virtually his entire life; Ames's young wife, Lila, whom he married in later years, and their six-year-old son, Robby; Ames's best friend, Robert Boughton, who is the pastor of Gilead's Presbyterian church; Boughton's beloved son and Ames's namesake, John Ames Boughton, the antihero whose failings and spiritual struggles occasion most of the book's central conflicts

Plot summary: At age seventy-six, Rev. John Ames III knows that his heart is failing. Anxious to pass on a legacy of faith to his only son—a legacy his son is too young to receive—Ames begins to "write his begats" and to recount lessons he has learned from a life in ministry. His genealogy includes a fiery, visionary abolitionist preacher (Ames's grandfather), a pacifist minister who rebelled against his father's militant Christianity (Ames's father), and a brilliant scholar whose theology was liberalized by graduate studies in Germany (Ames's brother Edward). But the family history is overtaken by the unexpected arrival of John Ames Boughton, age forty-three, who has been away from Gilead for twenty years. Jack, as he is called, is the proverbial prodigal son (also Ames's godson). Though loved beyond anything he deserves, Jack has humiliated his family in the past by (among other things) fathering the child of a local farm girl. He returns to Gilead with another secret, which he discloses only to Ames: a common-law wife and son ("colored") in Mississippi. Ames wrestles with his aggravation over Jack's misconduct and with his own sense of guilt for not loving his godson or giving him the pastoral direction he needs and almost seems to desire. Does God still have grace for this wayward son? Throughout *Gilead*, Ames writes with a constant awareness of his own mortality; he is saying farewell to the life, the family, and the ministry he loves.

of liberalism and abandons Christian orthodoxy. As a matter of conscience, when Edward returns home for vacation, he cannot even say grace at the family dinner table.

The son who remains at home all his life—at home both in the humble town of Gilead and in the practice of old-time Protestant religion—is Rev.

John Ames III. Though he is well aware of various intellectual attacks against Christianity, Ames steadfastly perseveres to the end of his ministry, leaving behind a legacy of faith.

A Life in Ministry

Gilead is an epistolary novel, written by a pastor in his seventies to a son who is too young to receive all the wisdom that an old man wants to share. So Ames writes his son a long letter that includes important episodes in family history, summaries of important sermons, practical admonitions for daily life, digressions on topics of theological interest, and many expressions of personal affection.

Ames writes to share with his son "things I would have told you if you had grown up with me," with the goal of leaving "a reasonably candid testament to my better self." The minister is not without his faults, of course, including some that he openly acknowledges (like his covetousness or his difficulties in loving the people he is called to pastor) and some that are apparent only to the reader (his racism, for example, as revealed in his casual dismissal of a black congregation that left Gilead after its building was damaged by arson). But Ames also bears witness to his "better self." He is an admirable man, whose ministry upholds many of the highest ideals of gospel ministry. Thus, *Gilead* presents one of the more positive portrayals of pastoral ministry in world literature.

Ames's pastorate is a ministry of the Word, sacraments, and prayer. He views ministry first in terms of preaching. Early in the novel we learn that he has kept all of his old sermon notes up in the attic. "Pretty nearly my whole life's work is in those boxes," he says. Ames estimates that at a rate of at least 50 sermons a year for 45 years, there must be 2,250 sermons in all. Written out in full, they amount to more than 67,000 pages, which he guesses is as much as Augustine or Calvin wrote. With a sense of legitimate satisfaction, not ungodly pride, Ames can testify that each of these sermons was preached with genuine conviction, for he believed that "a good sermon is one side of a passionate conversation." At appropriate points in his letter, the minister recounts the main argument from one of his sermons. From these homiletical digests, we sense his relish for working with the details of a biblical text, as well as his tendency to interpret Scripture partly through the lens of personal experience and reflection.

Ames is a minister of the sacrament as well as the Word. His sense of sacramental mystery was awakened in childhood when his father brought him a biscuit covered with ash out of the ruins of a church that had been struck by lightning—an incident he regards as his first communion. He later came to regard the sacrament of the Lord's Supper as a witness to the unity of the body of Christ, showing that the church anywhere is part of the church everywhere. Since he has spent virtually his entire life in a cultural backwater, his experience of the church is sheltered and parochial . . . "unless it really is a universal and transcendent life, unless the bread is the bread and the cup is the cup everywhere, in all circumstances, as I deeply believe."

Images of baptism recur throughout *Gilead*. Water itself seems miraculous to Ames, and key episodes in the novel occur while it is raining, or with some other glistening affusion. Ames remembers the baptism of Lila, who later became his wife, with a sense of mystery and sacred wonder ("What have I done? What does it mean?"). He also remembers the many newborns he baptized, "that feeling of a baby's brow against the palm of your hand—how I have loved this life." He regards baptism as a real blessing, in which water establishes an electric connection between the pastor and his parishioner, operating as "a vehicle of the Holy Spirit."

As much as anything else, Ames's ministry is a life of prayer. "I pray all the time," he claims, and this proves not to be an idle boast. *Gilead* is suffused with petitionary prayer. As a minister through two World Wars and one Great Depression, Ames often prayed over the "dreadful things" that his people were facing. Various sections of the letter end by mentioning matters that call for more prayer, and Ames sometimes leaves off his writing to go and pray. At night he walks the streets of Gilead and prays for people in their homes: "I'd imagine peace they didn't expect and couldn't account for descending on their illness or their quarreling or their dreams. Then I'd go into the church and pray some more and wait for daylight." The pastor's prayers are a means of grace for the people of God. His last words (also the closing line of the novel, as well as a famous quotation uttered by the titular character of Shakespeare's *King Lear*), form an appropriate epitaph: "I'll pray, and then I'll sleep."

FOR REFLECTION OR DISCUSSION

The Word, the sacraments, and prayer are fundamental to the ministry of any church. What relative priority do these practices have in your own congregation? What experiences in life or worship have helped you come to a deeper understanding of the mysteries of baptism and the Lord's Supper? How has participation in ministry helped you grow in the life of prayer?

Lessons Learned

One of Marilynne Robinson's extraordinary accomplishments in *Gilead* is to establish, as a woman, a plausible narrative voice for a man. Further, as a layperson she manages to capture with remarkable authenticity the interior life of a man who serves in pastoral ministry.

Ames is honest about the challenges of ministry, familiar to any pastor. He complains about church meetings ("just a few people came, and absolutely nothing was accomplished"). He confesses how hard it is to love his sheep ("After a while I did begin to wonder if I liked the church better with no people in it"). At the same time, Ames knows that his parishioners treat him differently, giving him more respect than he deserves—a "kindly imagining" that it is difficult for him to disillusion. He also laments the relentless approach of next week's sermon ("it seems to be Sunday all the time, or Saturday night. You just finish preparing for one week and it's already the next week").

With these inevitable challenges come many opportunities for personal ministry. The same people who suddenly change the subject when they see the minister coming, Ames says, will "come into your study and tell you the most remarkable things"—the dread, the guilt, and the loneliness that lie under the surface of life. In each pastoral encounter, he has sought to discern what the Lord is asking of him "in this moment, in this situation." Even if he has to deal with someone who is difficult, that person is "an emissary sent from the Lord" who affords him "the chance to show that I do in some small degree participate in the grace that saved me."

Over the course of a lifetime in ministry, addressing a wide range of spiritual needs, Ames has learned that trying to prove the existence of God is an ineffective strategy for dealing with spiritual doubt. "Nothing true can be said about God from a posture of defense," he believes. In fact, "the attempt to defend belief can unsettle it" because "there is always an inadequacy in argument about ultimate things." He has also learned how to answer the questions that people have about the torment of hell, which he believes the Bible characterizes primarily as separation from God: "If you want to inform yourselves as to the nature of hell, don't hold your hand in a candle flame, just ponder the meanest, most desolate place in your soul."

Ames has also learned the value of friendship for ministry. He is blessed to have Robert Boughton as his oldest, dearest friend and closest colleague in ministry. Having grown up together in Gilead, the two men now serve as pastors of the town's leading churches. They do not work in isolation but share ideas, discuss their sermons, and pray for one another's families.

FOR REFLECTION OR DISCUSSION

What are the hardest challenges you face as you serve God in the church? What are the most important lessons you have learned about ministry— the first lessons you would pass along to someone who is just starting out? What are the most common questions people ask about God? How have you learned to answer them (or not to answer them)?

Prodigal Grace

One of the great loves of Robert Boughton's life—and also his greatest grief—is his son Jack. Here Robinson views a familiar character-type from a fresh vantage point. We do not see the prodigal son from the perspective of his father but of his father's best friend. John Ames, too, has a fatherly role in Jack's life (the young man is his godson), but he stands more in the position of the older brother (see Luke 15:11–32). Ames describes himself as the good son who never left his father's house, "one of those righteous for whom the rejoicing in heaven will be comparatively restrained" (see Luke 15:7).

Like the older brother in the parable of the prodigal son, Ames resents Jack's careless immorality. "I don't know how one boy could have caused so much disappointment," he says, "without ever giving anyone any grounds for hope." For as long as Ames can remember, there has been something "devilish" about the boy's petty thefts and other sly transgressions. Jack's juvenile pranks were not fun-loving but mean-spirited. His greatest sin of all was to father the child of a poor country girl out of wedlock and then to neglect the child, who died of a common infection. The guilty charity of the rest of the Boughton family came too late to save her. "It was just terrible what happened to her," Ames says, "and that's a fact."

Ames believes that "the grace of God is sufficient to any transgression." He believes further that Boughton's love for his wayward son—"the most beloved"—exemplifies Christlike compassion. Yet he is also angered by the extravagance of his friend's fatherly affection, which he regards as overindulgence. Given the chance, Boughton would pardon every last one of his son's transgressions, past, present, and future. Ames finds it hard not to resent this, even though he knows that his feelings are at odds with his theology: "I have said at least once a week my whole adult life that there is an absolute disjunction between our Father's love and our deserving. Still, when I see this same disjunction between human parents and children, it always irritates me."

Ames's struggle to reconcile the true gravity of human sin with the free grace of God's forgiveness is complicated by his unique role in Jack's life. The boy was born long before Ames had a son of his own, and as a gift of Christian friendship, Boughton named him John Ames. Jack is Ames's namesake, his alter ego; indeed, he is "another self, a more cherished self." Yet when Ames performed Jack's baptism, he found his heart strangely cold toward the child. To his own guilt and shame, he has always found it difficult to love his godson the way his friend intended, or the way he knows a godly pastor should. He regards his namesake as possibly dangerous (where will Jack's growing friendship with Lila and Robby lead?) and probably dishonorable—someone who will "never really repent and never really reform." "I don't forgive him," Ames says. "I wouldn't know where to begin."

Like Ames, Jack Boughton fears that he is beyond forgiveness. Although he is an agnostic ("a state of categorical unbelief," he calls it: "I don't even believe God doesn't exist"), Jack still wonders whether there is any grace for him. This is the personal issue that lies behind the philosophical question he asks about predestination in one of the book's central dialogues: "Do you think some people are intentionally and irretrievably consigned to perdition?" Both Ames and Boughton err in taking this question as primarily theological rather than intensely pastoral. But Jack is really asking about himself: can he be saved, or is he beyond any hope of redemption? Surprisingly, it is Lila—not the ministers—who understands the real question and gives the most helpful response: "A person can change. Everything can change."

If Ames fails to give Jack the spiritual help he needs, it is not without misgivings. He believes that he is called to save the prodigal son and give him grace, that "ecstatic fire," but he is struggling within his soul: "I regret absolutely that I cannot speak with him in a way becoming a pastor." Ames begins to wish that somehow he could make up for the boy's cold baptism, that he could "put my hand on his brow and calm away all the guilt." Given the circumstances, he does the only thing he knows how to do and prays for Jack, asking God for the wisdom to care for him as a good shepherd.

These prayers are answered in the novel's climactic scene, which brings the balm to *Gilead*. After revealing that he has a "colored" wife and son, Jack decides to leave Gilead for good, even though it means abandoning his father in his dying days—a sin Ames knows that "only his father would forgive him for." Ames meets Jack at the bus station and asks to bless him, to pray for God's protection and pronounce a final benediction: "Lord, bless John Ames Boughton, this beloved son and brother and husband and father." These are loving words of the prodigal grace God lavishes on all prodigal sons. For Ames, to utter them on behalf of his namesake is worth seminary and ordination and all his years in ministry.

FOR REFLECTION OR DISCUSSION

All of the father-son relationships in Gilead *are marked by some form of estrangement or abandonment. According to Ames, "A man can know his father, or his son, and there might still be nothing between them but loyalty and love and mutual incomprehension." This is true for Ames himself, whose father cannot understand why he stays in Gilead, and whose son is too young to comprehend most of what his father wants to communicate. How has your relationship with your father (or some other family member) hindered your spiritual progress or helped you understand the grace of God? How can a father lavish grace on his children without excusing their sins or becoming overindulgent? Who are some of the prodigal sons and daughters on your prayer list? Where have you seen God's grace at work to restore children who have wandered away from him?*

Last Testament

From the beginning of his letter, Ames has known that soon he will have to leave behind his church, his family, and his very life. Marilynne Robinson deftly shows us signs of the patriarch's imminent mortality, through his growing need for sleep, through other physical symptoms, and through the solicitous concern of people who are waiting for him to die. Ames has even begun to write his funeral sermon, hoping to save old Boughton the trouble.

With death approaching, Ames reminisces about the past, which he describes honestly and poignantly without lapsing into undue sentimentality. He speaks of his love for his wife, the gracious gift of a son, and many other pleasures, including the joys and blessings of pastoral ministry. "Oh, I will miss the world!" he says. "Wherever you turn your eyes, the world can shine like transfiguration," as the "Lord breathes on this poor grey ember of Creation and it turns to radiance."

Ames also has more than a few regrets, as any minister does—"the frustrations and the disappointments of life, of which there are a very great many." He often wonders whether any of his sermons "were worth anything" and fears that he has been "boring a lot of people for a long time." He wishes, in fact, that his old sermon notes (an image of his own mortality) will be burned. He has often "known, right there in the pulpit, even as I read the words, how far they fell short of any hopes I had for them. And they were the major work of my life, from a certain point of view." He also regrets his failure, at times, to offer the best spiritual counsel: "I still wake up at night, thinking, *That's what I should have said!*" But his biggest regret, by far, is to leave behind his wife and son. Sadly, he will not be able to provide for their needs or to share life with them as they grow up and grow old.

In dealing with these regrets, Ames sees two choices: "(1) to torment myself or (2) to trust the Lord." Hoping to die "with a quiet heart," he chooses to place his ministry, his family, and his own life into God's hands. Rather than foolishly imagining that his congregation will be unable to manage without him, he preaches that Christ himself will be the pastor of his people. As for his son, he practices what he earlier preached from the story of Abraham and Ishmael, that "any father must finally give his child up to the wilderness and trust to the providence of God."

Thus ends the life of a faithful minister, who tried to keep the gospel before him as a standard for life and preaching and who remained loyal to his calling in a single church for nearly fifty years. Gilead is the town where he was born and also the town from which he will leave for home. "I think sometimes of going into the ground here as a last wild gesture of love," Ames writes near the end of his letter. "I too will smolder away the time until the great and general incandescence."

For Reflection or Discussion

Christ calls every one of his followers not simply to live well but also to die well, with "a quiet heart." Who are the pastors, ministry leaders, and other Christian servants whom you have seen finish strong in life and ministry? What habits or commitments enabled them to persevere? In what ways are you passing on a legacy of faith to others? How are you preparing to finish well?

PART 2

A Handbook of Literary
Portrayals of the Pastor's Life

Introduction

The pages that follow contain fifty-eight entries on works of literature that include significant discussion of a minister and illuminate issues in ministry. The entries have three goals: (1) to define the canon of works that portray and explore the role of the minister; (2) to provide enough information about each work to enable individual readers or discussion groups to decide if they wish to explore the work; (3) to give hints about how to interpret and discuss the work.

The guiding principles in selecting the works for the handbook were two: a book needed to (1) give major and not passing coverage to the clerical figure in the story and (2) clarify issues in ministry. The following scholarly sources can serve as a guide to anyone who wishes to cast a wider net than the handbook section of this book has done: Horton Davies, *A Mirror of the Ministry in Modern Novels* (New York: Oxford University Press, 1959); David Glenn Davis, "The Image of the Minister in American Fiction" (PhD dissertation, University of Tulsa, 1978); Raymond Chapman, compiler, *Godly and Righteous, Peevish and Perverse* (Grand Rapids: Eerdmans, 2002); G. Lee Ramsey Jr., *Preachers and Misfits, Prophets and Thieves: The Minister in Southern Fiction* (Louisville: Westminster John Knox, 2008).

The composition of the handbook was made possible by a small army of enthusiastic readers and codifiers of what they had read. We hereby gratefully record the names of contributors (listed alphabetically): Jill Peláez Baumgaertner, Margaret Ryken Beaird, Jake Boer, Linda Boice, Marion Clark, Ligon Duncan, Marie Friesema, Wendell Hawley, Heather House, Paul House, Barbara Hughes, Joel Lawrence, Laura Mail, Wayne Martindale, Amy Martinez, Doug O'Donnell, Rick Phillips, Melody Pugh, Carol Reid, Garnett Reid, Jacob Rhode, Jerry Root, Kelly Rose, Molly Rose, Chris Smith, Adam Snyder, Lorraine Triggs, Wil Triggs, and Elizabeth Vogel. Yee Sum Lo both contributed to the handbook and did a major share of the editing of the entries; we accordingly record a particular debt of gratitude to her.

Adam Bede

Author: George Eliot (pen name of Mary Ann Evans) (1819–80)

Nationality: English

Date of first publication: 1859

Approximate number of pages: 600

Available editions: numerous editions

Genres: novel, historical fiction

Setting for the story: the fictional community of Hayslope, a rural and pastoral town in 1799

Main characters: Hetty Sorrel, an eligible woman; Captain Arthur Donnithorne, the young squire who seduces Hetty; Adam Bede, another suitor; Dinah Morris, Hetty's cousin and a Methodist lay preacher; Mr. Irwine, the local Anglican minister

Plot summary: Adam Bede is a strong and virtuous laborer, but his one fault is that his heart is set on the immature but captivating Hetty. Hetty's desire, however, is fixed on the young squire Arthur Donnithorne, who loves Hetty and leads her to believe he will marry her, even though his place in society would never allow for such a union. In the end, Arthur's deception brings tragedy upon Hetty, Adam, and all those whose lives are bound in various ways to theirs.

In this her first novel, Eliot's expertise in laying open the human heart is evident as she tells the story of a sturdy and respected tradesman, Adam Bede, and the young woman he loves, Hetty Sorrel. But it is her depiction of two clergy, the solid and unobtrusive Mr. Irwine and the warm and loving Dinah Morris, that gives shape to the novel. Mr. Irwine is a stately clergyman of the Church of England who had ministered in Broxton for many years and had earned a deep respect, though not an abiding love, from his parishioners. Eliot's portrayal of Irwine is one of strength and solidity, and he serves as a moral compass in the midst of Donnithorne's unscrupulous behavior toward Hetty.

But the more important figure is Dinah. Filled with love and purity, she functions as a foil to Hetty. While Hetty is silly and selfish, Dinah is serious and filled with concern for those most in need of God's love. When Hetty finds herself arrested and imprisoned toward the climax of the novel, it is Dinah who runs to her, ministering to this proud, frightened young girl facing immense suffering. Dinah's presence in the prison cell mediates the presence of God.

She consoles and comforts Hetty in her hour of affliction and leads her to the release of confession that comes with throwing oneself on the mercy of God.

Mr. Irwine and Dinah are thus portrayed as ministers who represent, respectively, the Church of England and Methodism, and each demonstrates the characteristics of his or her church: Mr. Irwine is solid, grounded, not full of emotion and zeal but a harbor in the storm, while Dinah is dynamic, sensitive, and full of the love of God, which makes her a consoling presence in the midst of agony.

And the Shofar Blew

Author: Francine Rivers (1947–)

Nationality: American

Date of first publication: 1976

Approximate number of pages: 450

Available edition: Tyndale House

Genres: novel, Christian fiction

Setting for the story: Centerville, California

Main characters: Paul Hudson, pastor and protagonist; Eunice and Timothy, his wife and son; Samuel and Abigail Mason, faithful church members; Stephen Decker, church member, contractor for church construction, and alcoholic; David and Lois Hudson, parents of Paul (David is pastor of a large megachurch whose services are televised)

Plot summary: When gifted pastor Paul Hudson arrives at Centerville Christian Church, his ambitious plans for church growth quickly bypass the objections of the church's elderly leadership. His wife, Eunice, is tuned to spiritual things, but she cannot overcome the breach with older church members nor with her own son, who eventually resents his father's distance and harshness and leaves home. Stephen Decker first sees his work as architect and contractor for the new church building as an offering to God, but he resigns because of the financial misdealing of the new church leadership. When Eunice learns of Paul's affair with the wife of a wealthy and shallow church leader, she refuses to cover it up, leading to Paul's repentance and resignation from the church.

Paul Hudson is motivated more by his need for approval from his powerful and influential earthly father than by his need for approval from his heavenly

Father. His ambition for a large church causes him to discard solid Bible teaching, transparent relationships with godly leaders, Christian principles, and even his own family. He cannot see his father's weaknesses—the extramarital affairs, the public deceptions—until after his own infidelities are revealed.

Hudson stands in sharp contrast to Stephen Decker. Decker, a talented architect and contractor, has been divorced by his shrewish wife and has spent time in an alcohol recovery program. He craves more time with his daughter and wants her to know the Lord. He refuses temptation, both for alcohol and an affair, and his business dealings are entirely ethical and upstanding. He hungers for a deeper knowledge of Scripture and loves to share the gospel but is reluctant to answer the call to pastor a fellowship of believers. He is open to counsel and dependent on prayer. In the end, his humble faithfulness is rewarded, while the arrogant and prideful Paul Hudson is brought down.

Likewise, Eunice's commitment to holiness contrasts with her mother-in-law's desire for peace and reputation. The shofar's warning of danger and call to accountability ring clearly for the Hudson family.

At Home in Mitford

Author: Jan Karon (1937–)

Nationality: American

Date of first publication: 1994

Approximate number of pages: 400

Available edition: Penguin

Genres: novel, religious fiction

Setting for the story: Mitford, North Carolina

Main characters: Father Tim Kavanaugh, a sixty-year-old, unmarried Episcopal priest at Lord's Chapel Church; Dooley Barlowe, an abandoned mountain boy who becomes Father Tim's son; Cynthia Coppersmith, neighbor to the rectory

Plot summary: Father Tim's interactions with the members of his parish and his community are the primary focus in this book. However, several distinct story lines involve the bachelor priest's finding a family in a relationship with a stray dog, a vagabond boy, and a lovely new neighbor. He solves the riddle of missing jewels, the man in the attic, and Miss Sadie's lost love. He lays plans to minister to homeless men and build a new nursing home. His diabetic crisis calls him to a new perspective regarding his work and relationships.

Father Tim would be many people's idea of the perfect pastor. His words are delightfully well chosen and sweet; his faithfulness to his parishioners and community is comforting; his struggles with the everyday difficulties of life are realistic and thoughtful, always emphasizing the help of the heavenly Father.

Nine full-length novels published by Viking between 1994 and 2005 comprise the Mitford Years series. The titles are as follows: *At Home in Mitford*; *A Light in the Window*; *These High Green Hills*; *Out to Canaan*; *A New Song*; *A Common Life: The Wedding Story*; *In This Mountain*; *Shepherds Abiding*; and *Light from Heaven*. Karon's later series of books continues the characters' experiences away from Mitford, beginning with *Home to Holly Springs* (2008) and *Party of Four* (2010).

Several themes continue throughout the series, especially the themes of locating Dooley's family, Father Tim's physical and emotional health, his joyous relationship with Cynthia, and his ministry to his community. Father Tim takes on challenges in other parishes and eventually retires.

In a series this expansive, it is not surprising that the list of issues in ministry portrayed is also robust. The list includes the following: ministry to a congregation in a small town; working with a church secretary; ministerial call; ministerial burnout; serving as an unmarried minister; leaving a congregation; retiring from ministry; dealing with such parishioners' needs as mental illness, dying, grieving, and doubting; the minister as social worker; and resisting sexual advances from a parishioner.

Barchester Towers

Author: Anthony Trollope (1815–82)

Nationality: English

Date of first publication: 1857

Approximate number of pages: 300 (some editions 400)

Available editions: numerous editions

Genres: religious fiction, Victorian novel

Setting for the story: Barchester, a cathedral town in the west of England

Main characters: Dr. and Mrs. Proudie, the new bishop of Barchester and his wife; Rev. Obadiah Slope, ambitious chaplain of the Barchester church; Rev. Septimus Harding, former warden of Hiram's Hospital; Archdeacon Grantly, head of the high church forces and son-in-law of Rev. Harding; some of these characters also appear in Trollope's novel *The Warden*

Plot summary: This novel details the contest between Mrs. Proudie (the bishop's wife) and Rev. Slope (the bishop's chaplain) for primacy in the diocese. This sets the backdrop for the main conflict between the traditional high church forces and the new low church force. Both forces contend for the newly vacant post of warden of Hiram's Hospital. A major subplot concerns Slope's unsuccessful attempts to marry into money.

The portrayal of clergymen and their family members, intimately involved in the religious life of the region, is the focus of this novel. Major characters include Bishop and Mrs. Proudie, self-referential and utilitarian; the large family of Rev. Quiverful, fighting simply to survive; and Rev. Septimus Harding, formerly the warden of Hiram's Hospital, a principled man, unique in his world. While many men of principle are quick to reference their own principles as a means for judging the scruples of others, Harding finds greater profit in scrutinizing his own behavior and shortcomings. He is full of humility and gentleness. The reverse is true of his son-in-law, Archdeacon Grantly. His life is full of crusades, most of them designed to protect his own interests. The bishop's chaplain is Rev. Obadiah Slope, a man who recently added an *e* to his last name. He is pretentious and self-serving, and his entire life consists of adding *e*'s to things in the hopes of making them look better than they are.

Anthony Trollope weaves these characters into a tapestry that provides a map for making sense of the complex interactions of persons, which is so much a part of the church's topography. A person in ministry can learn much from a study of each of these characters. Trollope calls his readers to remember that only the preacher can compel people to sit still and be tortured. He also reminds those in ministry that proclamation, though persuasive, can be manipulative. How does one persuade while avoiding coercion? It is an art necessary to learn while doing ministry in a world not unlike Barchester, where people need nurturing in order to learn and grow in grace.

The Bishop's Mantle

Author: Agnes Sligh Turnbull (1888–1982)

Nationality: American

Date of first publication: 1947

Approximate number of pages: 360

Available edition: out of print but obtainable from used-book sources and libraries

Genres: novel, contemporary fiction, coming-of-age story

Setting for the story: a mid-Atlantic American city, possibly New York, in the late 1930s and early 1940s, focusing on a large Episcopal church and its parish against the backdrop of World War II

Main characters: Hilary Laurens, the young, idealistic rector of St. Matthew's; Lexa Laurens, the beautiful, wealthy, party-loving fiancée and later wife of Hilary; Dick Laurens, brother of Hilary and an unbeliever

Plot summary: A young minister mourns the loss of his uncle, the bishop of the church, and assumes the "bishop's mantle," beginning his ministry in the large urban congregation. As he takes on the challenges that come with his new position, he struggles in numerous personal relationships. Finally, the characters mature and come to terms with themselves and are ultimately reconciled with the roles they play.

When Hilary Laurens becomes rector of a prestigious Protestant Episcopal church, he is eager to follow his uncle's example of godly pastoral leadership. He has a love for the services and rituals of the church and a warm personal piety. He is willing to respond to emergencies and pleas for help, even in the middle of the night, and yearns to see his wealthy church become a place where the poor can also come, feel at home, and be ministered to. His idealism and sincere motives meet with misunderstandings, entrenched opinions, and downright sinful behavior on the part of some of his vestry members and parishioners.

Hilary's ministry is also complicated by the wife he adores and who seems to have no interest in anything remotely spiritual. The author has made a clear effort to portray a member of the clergy as a real man, dedicated and self-sacrificing, but also fallible and sometimes distracted by family problems and personal vulnerabilities.

The rector impresses his congregation and begins to attract doubters and skeptics—such as a bright, agnostic doctor—with thought-provoking sermons. But these sermons are built on higher criticism's skeptical view of Scripture. Hilary's self-giving ministry coexists with the basic liberalism of many mainline churches of the mid-twentieth century. This competently written novel combines a high view of the calling and self-sacrifice of Christian pastoral service with a low view of the truths and doctrines of orthodox biblical Christianity.

The Book against God

Author: James Wood (1965–)

Nationality: English

Date of first publication: 2003

Approximate number of pages: 260

Available edition: Farrar, Straus and Giroux

Genres: novel, domestic fiction

Settings for the story: London; Sundershall, England

Main character: Thomas Bunting, an atheist philosophy student

Plot summary: Thomas Bunting reflects on his unraveled life as he tries to reunite with his wife, attempts to understand his relationship with his deceased father, and struggles to live life without restraint.

Thomas Bunting is a reflexive liar. He lies to his wife about having paid the bills. He lies to his minister father about his faith. He lies to his mother about his doctoral research. He lies to himself about why his life is in its current state. In an attempt to understand how things have gone so wrong, Thomas examines the events of the last year to see what prompted his wife to leave him, how it happened that his father died believing that Thomas was searching for a relationship with Jesus, when in fact he is an avowed secularist, and how his philosophical degree was derailed by devotion to a new project, a compilation that Thomas calls "The Book against God."

Convinced that God does not exist, Thomas becomes preoccupied with writing "The Book against God," a manifesto that records antireligious quotations by thinkers through the ages as well as Thomas's own arguments about philosophical and religious matters. The four-volume diatribe seems to provide an outlet for confessing his own unbelief, which he cannot bring himself to admit to his father, a devout Anglican minister. He craves his father's approval but seems utterly incapable of enjoying the very things that mark his father's life: a happy marriage, a solid character, a sure direction, and a trusting faith.

Thomas's wife was waiting for him to complete his doctoral work, thinking they could then start a family. His parents were anxious for him to finish his degree and live out a personal commitment to Christ, thinking a job could provide stability and faith could provide direction. Thomas's work on "The Book against God" becomes his consuming expression of his faithlessness and, conveniently, a backhanded way to thwart his parents' and his wife's desires for his life.

While his childish behaviors do not always bear this out, Thomas loves his wife and wants to please his parents. He believes his current difficulties would be solved if his wife would take him off marital probation and if he could pursue his philosophical ponderings free of dissertation stress or employment responsibilities. But without a father to please and resist, he cannot make his life meaningful.

<hr />

The Book of Bebb

Author: Frederick Buechner (1926–)

Nationality: American

Date of first publication: 1979

Approximate number of pages: 530

Available edition: HarperOne; *The Book of Bebb* is a tetralogy whose individual books include: *Lion Country* (1971), *Open Heart* (1972), *Love Feast* (1974), and *Treasure Hunt* (1977)

Genres: novel, comedy, picaresque novel, religious satire

Settings for the story: Florida, Texas, New York City, and South Carolina in the late 1960s

Main characters: Leo Bebb, a charlatan evangelist/minister; Antonio Parr, an English teacher and narrator of the story; Sharon Bebb, Leo's adopted daughter who marries Antonio; Lucille, Bebb's alcoholic wife; Gertrude Conover, Bebb's rich octogenarian theosophist companion; Babe, Bebb's twin brother

Plot summary: Antonio answers Leo Bebb's ad to ordain anyone who sends a love offering. He intends to expose the charlatan minister's work at Holy Love Church in Florida but ends up as Bebb's son-in-law. Bebb also ordains a wealthy Indian, Herman Redpath, who dies and leaves Bebb with a fortune to continue his scam of a ministry. Bebb continues to run from his past and the IRS. He and Lucille move to New York to be near Bebb's daughter, Sharon, and to start a new church, named Open Heart, which Bebb's former cell mate burns down. Lucille drowns her depression with alcohol and commits suicide. Meanwhile, Antonio struggles with his wife's infidelity, which destroys their marriage. Bebb finds a new companion and benefactor in Gertrude Conover, who helps him stage a love feast for the college crowd at Princeton. When the university refuses to let him continue meeting on campus, Bebb stages a stunt that costs him his life and sends his family and friends on a treasure hunt, resulting in an encounter with Bebb's long-lost twin, Babe. They discover the truth about Bebb and his family's past.

Bebb wants to "do something big for Jesus" by selling Bibles, but this is not big enough for him. So he becomes a self-proclaimed preacher, faith healer, evangelist, and theologian, using proof texts and emotional appeals to fleece the weak-minded, vulnerable, and rich in order to recruit followers and fund his scams. To a minister as flamboyant as Bebb, image is everything, so he hides his sordid past behind "Gospelese" and benevolent acts. His story is about wrong motives and wrong methods in ministry. His call for repentance is actually a sermon to self. Other characters in the story show that without firm beliefs people can fall for anything, including a charismatic figure like Bebb.

The story raises the following issues in ministry: using one's ministry to escape from and rectify one's past, using proof texts from the Bible to justify one's actions with no accountability, placing ministry ahead of family, and presenting the gospel through outlandish and sometimes fraudulent means.

Brendan: A Novel

Author: Frederick Buechner (1926–)

Nationality: American

Date of first publication: 1988

Approximate number of pages: 240

Available editions: HarperOne, Kindle

Genres: novel, fictional biography (life of St. Brendan the Navigator [ca. 483–577]), saint's life

Setting for the story: fifth- to sixth-century Ireland

Main characters: Brendan, the celebrated Irish saint and explorer who lived a generation after St. Patrick and sailed in a leather "curragh," possibly as far as Florida; Bishop Erc, "weaned from druidry" by St. Patrick; Abbess Ita and Abbot

Jarlath, early formative influences on Brendan; Brendan's childhood companions: Maeve, a tomboy who emerges from the abbey not as a nun but as a warrior, and his traveling companion Finn, who is also the narrator of the book; Crosan and Colman, formerly clown and bard in the pagan kingdom of Cashel, along with three monks—Dismas, Gestas, and Malo—who largely fill out Brendan's crew of explorers

Plot summary: As a young child, Brendan is whisked off to an abbey, and when he comes of age, he is sent on a mission prior to being ordained as a priest. The mission is successful, as Brendan converts one pagan ruler to Christ and crowns the first Christian king over another formerly pagan realm. Upon returning home, Brendan decides to set out to sea in search of Tir-na-n-Og, the pagan "land of the blessed," which for Brendan is a syncretistic muddle of pagan and Christian visions of paradise. Brendan's two voyages and his founding of a monastic community make up the remainder of the story.

One of Frederick Buechner's greatest gifts is that he writes knee-deep in earth and incarnation. His portrait of Brendan is as earthy and raw as real life itself. Brendan lives in a world where the "new faith" is emerging, but that world is still thick with paganism, druids, and magic.

The story is not hero worship, however. Finn, the narrator, won't allow it to be. He tells the truth as he sees it and shows Brendan "warts and all." In fact, Finn is a bit skeptical after witnessing Brendan's sometimes outrageous and exaggerated claims. Finn also wonders if Brendan's bold chasing after God's glory is really an attempt to escape the guilt of his sin. That guilt, along with suffering and grief on the part of several other characters, brings up the question of the justice of God. In the middle of the novel, Brendan plays with the phrase "God is just," asking if he's heard correctly or whether it is really "God is jest." The question hovers over the rest of the novel. Is God just, or is he just playing a joke on us?

Questions about God's justice, despair over sin, the effects of grief, the value of deep friendship, and gospel boldness are all considered in ways that can benefit one's ministry.

Brideshead Revisited

Author: Evelyn Waugh (1903–66)

Nationality: English

Date of first publication: 1945

Approximate number of pages: 350

Available editions: numerous editions

Genres: satire, novel, literature of place, family saga, semiautobiographical novel (*Bildungsroman*), coming-of-age story

Settings for the story: London; Oxford; Brideshead Manor, Oxfordshire; the main action takes place between the World Wars, with the final action brought about because of World War II

Main characters: Charles Ryder, an agnostic painter; Sebastian Flyte, Charles's best friend; Julia Flyte, Sebastian's older sister and Charles's lover; Cordelia Flyte, Sebastian's younger sister; Lady Marchmain, Sebastian's mother; Lord Marchmain, Sebastian's absent father

Plot summary: Using a first-person narrative, the story follows Charles Ryder's spiritual awakening, brought about by his complex relationship with one of England's most established Catholic families. His visits to Brideshead enmesh him in the Marchmain family's problems, caused by the mother's conduct of religion. While much of the novel focuses on the characters' enjoyment of a life of excess and privilege, personal loss causes all of the characters to reckon with the difficult but necessary action of grace in their lives.

In *Brideshead Revisited*, three ministers represent the movement of grace in the lives of Charles, Sebastian, and Julia. During their early years at Oxford, Charles and Sebastian are caught up in a life of excess and privilege. At the same time, the minister Mr. Samgrass is presented as a tool of Lady Marchmain. Blinded by her wealth, he acts at her behest, spying on Sebastian and covering for the young men when their inappropriate behavior may reflect badly on the Marchmain family. All of these characters live a life that prioritizes material prosperity over spiritual depth.

When Sebastian seeks a spiritual vocation by traveling to North Africa, he finds refuge and medical care in a Tunisian monastery. The monks offer hope for those who suffer the long-term impact of choices made in desperation and despair. Rather than condemning people like Sebastian, they make a place in the midst of their spiritual community for those who long for but struggle to accept God's healing grace.

After the death of Lady Marchmain, Charles and Julia return to Brideshead, where they conduct an illicit affair. They are joined at the manor by Lord Marchmain, who has returned to the family home to die. Here, the novel introduces Father Mackay, who does not force faith on anyone or withdraw from those who struggle with faith. Instead, he waits patiently for Lord Marchmain's deathbed confession and readily responds to Julia when she calls for his intervention. Father Mackay anticipates the need for each person to encounter grace in his or her own time.

The Bridge of the San Luis Rey

Author: Thornton N. Wilder (1897–1975)

Nationality: American

Date of first publication: 1927

Approximate number of pages: 160

Available editions: HarperCollins, Penguin

Genre: novel

Setting for the story: Peru in the early years of the eighteenth century

Main characters: Brother Juniper, a Franciscan monk who undertakes six years of research into the lives of the five people who fell to their deaths when the bridge collapsed; the five victims of the catastrophe

Plot summary: The famous opening sentence of the novel asserts the central event in the story: "On Friday noon, July the twentieth, 1714, the finest bridge in all Peru broke and precipitated five travellers into the gulf below." The bridge was actually a flimsy footbridge ladder with slats, spanning a deep gorge. Brother Juniper witnessed the tragedy. Having long pondered the question of why tragedy befalls good people, he undertakes a six-year search into the lives of the five people who perished. The Spanish Inquisition declares Brother Juniper's conclusions heretical, and Brother Juniper is burned as a heretic.

The story creates such a sense of actuality that it is important to know that the central event and all but two of the characters were invented by the author. The three chapters devoted to the life stories of the five victims take on a life of their own and are seemingly unrelated to a central focus. There is a common thread, however: all five people were at a turning point and ready to begin a new life.

Brother Juniper, the clerical figure in the story, is not a dominant character, but he sets in motion the deeper meanings of the story. He represents a common feature of any minister's (or Christian's) life, namely, how to reconcile human catastrophe with one's providential view of life. The first and last chapters in the novel are "Perhaps an Accident" and "Perhaps an Intention." In other words, are disasters in life a product of chance or providence? Do the victims of disaster deserve it, thereby confirming the principle of justice? Or does disaster strike apart from human deserving? The novel itself does not clarify the conclusions to which Brother Juniper comes in his book, though the novel implies that he wanted to reach an orthodox viewpoint.

The book poses the issues of confronting the theological question of theodicy (reconciling God's goodness and sovereignty with the fact of human suffering) and also the oppression of a tyrannical institutional church, in this case the Spanish Inquisition.

The Brothers Karamazov

Author: Fyodor Dostoevsky (1821–81)

Nationality: Russian

Date of first publication: 1880

Approximate number of pages: 750

Available editions: numerous editions

Genres: philosophical novel, murder mystery, literature of place

Setting for the story: the relatively small Russian village of Skotoprigonyevsk in the 1860s, far removed from the influences of urban life and industrialization

Main characters: Fyodor Pavlovitch; his sons Ivan, Dimitri (also called Mitya), and Alyosha (also called Alexey); Smerdyakov, Fyodor's illegitimate son whose murder of his father becomes the focus of the action; Father Zossima, the elder of the town monastery

Plot summary: The novel tells the story of three brothers and the difficult events they encounter in a period of three months. Each of them faces personal suffering, ranging from the death of a mentor to the perceived betrayal of a lover, but it is their differing reactions—from rage to guilt to hope—that are most telling of their personalities. Ultimately, a brutal murder and the ensuing trial prompt exploration of the themes of justice, forgiveness, and eternal love.

While the overall aim of *The Brothers Karamazov* is to bring us into the lives of the entire Karamazov family, a couple of clerical characters emerge to add a spiritual dimension to the events of the novel. The only main character who is a cleric by profession is the elder Zossima, a spiritual leader and mentor in a Russian Orthodox monastery. His healing abilities, religious insight, and practical wisdom make him nearly universally loved and revered. Even the Karamazov family attempts to have Father Zossima mediate an argument, but their stubborn tempers render reconciliation impossible.

At the novel's opening, the youngest brother, Alyosha, lives at the monastery and has taken Father Zossima as his elder. Before Father Zossima dies, he commands Alyosha to leave the monastery and go into the world. Alyosha does so reluctantly and continues the ministry of his elder in the tumultuous world outside the monastery. Alyosha is the most pastorally active character in the novel, ministering both to his brothers and to others in his community. He befriends a group of schoolboys and is especially Christlike toward Kolya, the outcast in the group. His own family is his greatest mission field. In a particularly famous scene ("The Grand Inquisitor"), Alyosha's brother Ivan rejects him and Christ. Alyosha's spiritual purity leads to complexity in his relationships, as most of his acquaintances alternately love and hate him. Alyosha is the moral and spiritual compass of *The Brothers Karamazov*, and his relationships act as litmus tests for the judgment of moral success or failure of the other characters.

The Damnation of Theron Ware

Author: Harold Frederic (1856–98)

Nationality: American

Date of first publication: 1896

Approximate number of pages: 325

Available editions: Bibliolife, Standard Publications

Genres: novel; realistic, regional fiction

Setting for the story: Octavius, a fictional, Methodist town corresponding to Utica, New York

Main characters: Theron Ware, a young Methodist minister; Alice, his wife; Celia, a beautiful Catholic woman; Father Forbes, the Catholic priest; Dr. Ledsmar, a skeptical scientist; Candace Soulsby, a church fund-raiser

Plot summary: The story traces the descent of a Methodist minister, Theron Ware, from a promising pulpit career to being washed out of the ministry. Ware is "enlightened" by new friendships with a liberal Catholic priest, a scientific scholar, and a free-spirited woman. Their sophisticated knowledge leads him to disdain his comparatively plain and naive ministry, religion, and wife.

Theron Ware is a progressive young Methodist minister. He is gifted as an orator and expects to follow a rising path in the ministry. His supportive wife, Alice, shares his expectation. Ware is nevertheless assigned to a small, backward, and tightfisted church. His challenge is to last through the assignment, battle the hard-nosed trustees, and keep afloat financially until a better appointment comes.

The story takes a turn when Ware meets a Roman Catholic priest, a beautiful Catholic woman, and a scientific scholar. These three "illumine" Ware to sophistication, beauty, and knowledge. From Father Forbes and Dr. Ledsmar, Ware learns that the Bible is a book of myths. From Celia, he is awakened to beauty and passion. In his mind, he is being transformed and transported to a higher plane of living. All the while, his wife becomes duller, his religion seems primitive, and his ministry appears no more than a deception necessary to maintain a living.

The damnation of Ware does not come from the church but from his new friends. In his illusion of being transformed into a sophisticated being, he does not see that he is merely turning into an arrogant, superficial bore. He experiences their rejection and would have been undone if not for the rescue of Brother and Sister Soulsby. Through the efforts of these realists, he is somewhat restored, albeit out of the ministry and without restored faith or marital love. Ultimately, the damning flaw of Ware is that he never understands his own heart or the gospel, which must be the fate of moralistic ministers.

The Dean's Watch

Author: Elizabeth Goudge (1900–1984)

Nationality: English

Date of first publication: 1960

Approximate number of pages: 300

Available edition: out of print but obtainable from used-book sources and libraries

Genres: novel, regional or local-color writing, literature of place, Christmas story

Setting for the story: an unnamed cathedral town called "The City" (modeled on Ely, where the author lived for a time) in the 1870s; the world of the novel is a High Church Anglican world

Main characters: Adam Ayscough, dean of the cathedral; Isaac Peabody, the local maker and repairer of clocks and watches

Plot summary: The story portrays a slice of life in a cathedral town as numerous townspeople interact. They are mainly people oppressed within and without. Through interacting with one another they are mellowed by love. The action occurs during the final few months in the life of the dean, who dies the day after Christmas.

Although Dean Adam Ayscough has carried on a successful social reform of his cathedral town, he begins the story as the archetypal unpleasant cleric. He preaches boring sermons. His marriage to Elaine is a failure. He doesn't know how to relate to people. The watch that he regularly overwinds is his initial link to Isaac Peabody the watch repairer, an unhappy man who lives unpleasantly with his sister Emma. In fact, the entire city seems to be comprised of unloving, needy people.

The main action is the progress of grace in the city. The dean is as much the recipient as the agent of this movement of grace, and it is chiefly through his relationships with people that the transformation occurs. The movement starts when Peabody returns a repaired watch to the dean with the wrong note attached; the dean takes the four lines of poetic verse to heart and engages Peabody in conversation when he makes his weekly visit to the dean's house to set the clocks.

After this encounter, the story line portrays a gradual lessening of hatred among numerous unloving people of the town. The story traces how the dean manages to transform his own life and relationships and those of others, making it a case study in how to conduct a salvage operation in a minister's life and calling in a community. The focus is moral (loving people) rather than spiritual (relating to God), but the moving Christmas finale gives glimpses of a spiritual reality behind the moral reform.

Death Comes for the Archbishop

Author: Willa Cather (1873–1947)

Nationality: American

Date of first publication: 1927

Approximate number of pages: 350

Available editions: Modern Library, Vintage

Genres: novel, literature of place, regional or local-color writing

Setting for the story: the American frontier, 1848–88

Main characters: Father Jean Marie Latour, archbishop of New Mexico; Father Joseph Vaillant, longtime friend of Father Latour, missionary priest, and eventual bishop of Colorado

Plot summary: In 1848, longtime friends and ministry partners Father Jean Marie Latour and Father Joseph Vaillant are called from their posts as missionaries in the Great Lakes region to serve in the New Mexico Territory. For the next forty years, the two men crisscross the mountainous and desert terrain, establishing churches, fighting corruption, and making cultural inroads among the indigenous people, American and Mexican settlers. As the men age, they must grapple with changing times and shifting cultural norms, while also confronting their own mortality.

When Jean Marie Latour and Joseph Vaillant first ride into Santa Fe, they believe they have come to claim the New Mexico Territory for God. But the story emphasizes that any minister who seeks to change a community—its people or the place itself—will himself be irrevocably changed.

Though they have served many years together in Ohio, neither man is fully prepared for the challenges of the New Mexico Territory. Both men find themselves shaped by the determination it takes to withstand the arid environment. But just as the environment shapes them, they seek to shape the land: they teach the Mexican people to cultivate fruit trees and properly irrigate their land. Though the priests always reject traditional religious practices that do not fit within the bounds of Christian theology, they learn to respect the Mexican value of upholding tradition. In service of the church, they unseat the corrupt Mexican priests, but they continue to accept the ill-gotten gains of the Mexican landlords.

The missionary journeys to which Frs. Latour and Vaillant are called perpetuate the habits formed in their shared childhood: Father Vaillant remains a man of the people, beloved by all, while Father Latour carries the administrative and theological burdens. But in the bleak and often violent world of the frontier, the French priests are sustained not only by their devotion to the church but also by their friendship. Their reliance on one another's gifts is tested by the demands of the growing territory, but as they age, they discover that their enduring friendship has strengthened and deepened each man, preparing him to faithfully and ably fulfill his vocation.

◆◆◆

Death in Holy Orders

Author: P. D. James (1920–)

Nationality: English

Date of first publication: 2001

Approximate number of pages: 400

Available editions: Knopf, Ballantine, Fawcett

Genres: novel, detective fiction, mystery story

Setting for the story: the East Anglian coast of Britain, within the enclosed grounds of St. Anselm's Theological College, late twentieth century

Main characters: Police Commander Adam Dalgliesh; Detective Inspectors Kate Miskin and Piers Tarrant; Fathers John, Martin, and Peregrine, faculty members at St. Anselm's Theological College

Plot summary: The suspicious suicide of a young seminarian brings Commander Dalgliesh to St. Anselm's, but his inquiries are derailed when the archdeacon turns up murdered in the church. The ensuing investigation uncovers a complex web of secret relations within the seminary. The plot turns uniquely on the reliability of written texts, including the mysterious St. Anselm Papyrus, an ancient document that questions the resurrection of Christ.

The faculty members at St. Anselm's Theological College lead a life of routine and tradition, characterized by each man's unique contribution to this intentional Christian community. The teaching priests emphasize spiritual formation, intellectual development, the contemplative life, and maintenance of church tradition. When the atheist father of a student enlists Scotland Yard to investigate his son's apparent suicide, Dalgliesh returns to the college, where he spent many fond summers as a child. He finds that the daily routine of the seminary only thinly veils an increasing tension among the faculty and staff. The archdeacon, who sees a private seminary as increasingly irrelevant in modern culture, has threatened to close St. Anselm's and sell its assets.

While most detective novels begin with mystery and move to enlightenment, this story begins with confidence in human knowledge and a desire for human justice. But the investigation of the archdeacon's untimely death causes the faculty at St. Anselm's, and Dalgliesh himself, to question human notions of truth and justice. As both poet and detective, Dalgliesh trains his attention on understanding human nature and uncovering truth, which he believes will inevitably lead to justice. His confidante, Father Martin, encourages him to consider the complex question the priests must ask: should an enclosed community value truth at all costs over protecting its members from further harm? For Martin, the existence of the St. Anselm Papyrus serves as a metaphor for this question. The document, which questions the resurrection of Christ, pits divine revelation against human knowledge. As the facts of the case, and the document itself, are brought to light, each person involved must confront difficult questions about the relationship between human understanding and divine justice.

Deep River

Author: Shusaku Endo (1923–96)

Nationality: Japanese

Date of first publication: 1993

Approximate number of pages: 220

Available edition: New Directions

Genres: novel, religious fiction, regional writing

Setting for the story: the city of Varanasi along the Ganges River in India

Main characters: Otsu, a young Catholic priest who abandoned the priesthood while wrestling with his theology; Mitsuko, a newly divorced friend of Otsu looking for meaning in life; Osamu, a tourist seeking incarnation of his deceased wife; Kiguchi, a veteran seeking ritualistic cleansing; Numada, a Manchurian native who seeks answers in nature

Plot summary: The life stories of Japanese tourists intersect as they travel to the sacred Ganges River. All have had their own bitter experiences and are seeking answers to their adversities. When the Indian prime minister is assassinated, the tourists are swept into the resulting political and religious turmoil. Amid the drama, the Ganges River offers a spiritual resolution and peace to their individual journeys.

Otsu comes from a Christian family and has embraced faith all his life. As a young, talented university student, he endures teasing from Mitsuko; she mocks his faith in God and eventually seduces him. Though Otsu maintains his devotion to the church, he does so insecurely once Mitsuko rejects him. Despite her outward irreverence, Mitsuko inwardly admires Otsu and remains curious about his faith.

Otsu loses track of Mitsuko and moves to Lyon to study for the priesthood. Once again Otsu encounters his former lover, who is desperately seeking enlightenment for her dusky soul. She is now more vehement in her disdain for Christianity, which she labels "European nonsense." Otsu, however, defies her scorn and again confesses faith in God. Yet her protests have made their mark on Otsu's heart. In his correspondence with Mitsuko, the aspiring priest admits he has begun to doubt his faith. Though he will not renounce the church, he is drawn to Eastern religions. (This same conflict between Eastern and Western religions appears in Endo's more famous novel *Silence*.) He admires Christ's suffering but sees it as only part of a larger redemptive worldview. As Otsu carries corpses to the Ganges while living at a Hindu monastery in Varanasi, he detects a divinity within the sacred river purging and renewing all the oppressed who are immersed in it.

Otsu emerges as a conflicted figure, unwilling to leave the church but seeing Christ's burden-bearing fulfilled in his own portage of sorrowful souls to the Ganges. In the end, Otsu himself is mistakenly attacked in the place of another who is guilty. His experience thus echoes the messianic refrain from Isaiah 53 found throughout the story: "Surely he hath borne our griefs, and carried our sorrows."

Father Brown

Author: G. K. Chesterton (1874–1936)

Nationality: English

Date of first publication: 1911 as *The Innocence of Father Brown*

Approximate number of pages: 725 for complete works

Available editions: as an omnibus, *The Complete Father Brown*, from Penguin and Oxford; older collections are titled *The Innocence of Father Brown, The Wisdom of . . . , The Incredulity of . . . , The Secret of . . . ,* and *The Scandal of Father Brown*

Genres: crime story, mystery story, short story

Setting for the story: varied, but mostly in England

Main characters: Father Brown, a Catholic priest with uncanny insight into human evil; Flambeau, a reformed criminal

Plot summary: A variety of criminal cases are solved by the mild-mannered Father Brown through his penchant for detail, knowledge of the criminal mind (through hearing confession), and acute theological insights.

Father Brown is a "mild, hard-working little priest." The perspective of all those who meet him is summed up by the comment, "Everything seemed undistinguished about the priest." The catch is that the little priest has the mind of Sherlock Holmes, a character G. K. Chesterton admired. He possesses the same gifts of observation and deduction as Holmes and has amassed through his experience of the human heart the same propensity to think like a criminal.

But the dark cloud hanging over the brooding Detective Holmes is not present with the mild-mannered Father Brown, who is content in his priestly calling. He brings to his detective work the same pastoral care for both victim and criminal. Brown's clergy garb is not a disguise for an intelligent mind but rather its explanation. Hearing the confession of "men's real sins" gives him a thorough understanding of the criminal mind and the evil in men's hearts. But more to the point, it is his theological mind that sharpens his thinking.

The fifty-two short stories, which cover a wide variety of crimes, locations, and characters, make a fun read for all mystery lovers. The famous Chesterton wit adds further delight for those who appreciate a turn of phrase. Even so, it is the Christian Chesterton who comes through, as he does not miss an opportunity to take aim at atheists and secularists (and a few Calvinists). The detective priest is loosely based on the real priest Father John O'Connor, who had a role in Chesterton's conversion. But more than depicting a single priest, Father Brown is the embodiment of the church—of humble appearance, yet possessing inwardly the strength of mind and the theological insight to overcome evil and bring forth light.

The Flight of Peter Fromm

Author: Martin Gardner (1914–)

Nationality: American

Date of first publication: 1974

Approximate number of pages: 280

Available edition: Prometheus Books

Genres: semiautobiographical novel (*Bildungsroman*); coming-of-age story

Setting for the story: University of Chicago during the now-famous Hutchins-Adler period

Main characters: Peter Fromm, a divinity school student; Homer Wilson, a pastor and professor who serves as Peter's biographer and mentor

Plot summary: This is a coming-of-age story regarding the theology of one man. The novel depicts a traditionally Protestant Christian man struggling with his faith, examining twentieth-century scholarship and intellectual movements, and ultimately rejecting Christianity while remaining a theist.

Peter Fromm, who grew up in Sands Springs, Oklahoma, goes to the University of Chicago Divinity School, where he falls from the sandy and slippery foundation of his childhood faith. He moves from his early Pentecostal roots to an "enlightened" rejection of the doctrines of original sin, the virgin birth, the physical resurrection, and the blood atonement. This flight from the faith is the main action of the novel.

Homer Wilson, the narrator of the story, serves as the catalyst for Fromm's odyssey from orthodoxy. Fromm entered the divinity school as a reformer, called by God to cast out the demons of secular humanism. Yet Wilson, a Unitarian minister, adjunct professor, Freudian, communist sympathizer, and atheist, sets Fromm on the path to "truth." While Fromm never embraces Wilson's atheism, he certainly embraces many of his views on the Bible, Jesus, politics, and morality. Notably, each step away from traditional Christian thinking is also a step away from traditional Christian morality.

These steps are set within the context of Fromm's relationships with women and his reading of influential religious thinkers. Once Fromm has embraced the theory of evolution and subsequently abandoned his fundamentalist view of the Bible, he looks for a way to keep his orthodox faith. He dabbles with multiple perspectives, finally ending his quest with an abandonment of orthodoxy and an acceptance of Albert Schweitzer's Christology—a view that maintains Jesus was just a disillusioned man who saw himself as the Son of God.

The climax of the story is the depiction of Fromm's inward conflicts manifested outwardly during his Easter Sunday sermon on the verse "If Christ be not risen, then is our preaching vain, and your faith is also vain" (1 Cor. 15:14 KJV), ultimately concluding the narrative as a warning against religious hypocrisy, intellectual naiveté, and presumption. The novel shows the damage that comes when a poor theological upbringing makes a person unable to withstand challenges from professors and pastors who undermine the gospel.

The Gauntlet

Author: James Howell Street (1903–54)

Nationality: American

Date of first publication: 1945

Approximate number of pages: 310

Available edition: out of print but obtainable from used-book sources and libraries

Genres: novel, Christian fiction

Settings for the story: Linden, Missouri; Southwestern Baptist Theological Seminary, Texas

Main characters: London Wingo, a passionate but novice pastor; his wife, Kathie, a pastor's daughter and the voice of wisdom in the parsonage; Brother Honeycutt, the outgoing minister replaced by Wingo; Page Musselwhite, a fellow seminary student and Wingo's counselor

Plot summary: London Wingo drops out of seminary and takes on the pastorship of a small Missouri church when his wife gets pregnant. He wrestles with his own calling, pride, ambition, and faith as well as the domination over his life that his church members exert. He launches manipulative and successful programs in his ministry, but at the same time he gradually builds opposition, spite, and disrespect as the gauntlet to his role as preacher. His wife's sudden death serves as a wake-up call and begins the reconciliation between pastor and church.

When he begins his first pastorate in the small town of Linden, Missouri, London Wingo achieves instant popularity with his passionate sermons and handsome appearance. He courts the youth of the community and is progressive in instituting change while subtly giving the credit to others. He stands up against the threats of an influential but uneducated family leader in the church and gains still more respect.

But when the Wingos resist the powerful deacons and old guard of church leadership, painful rumors and personal attacks follow. The young couple overcomes these challenges, only to face more accusations and opposition in their wake. They plan to leave the small church for another pastorate in a larger town. Kathie's death becomes the climax to London's struggle.

Through the course of his fledgling ministry, London comes to grips with his own wavering faith, finally describing his philosophy of ministry as Christian humanism. The godly advice of his friend Page and the understanding of Brother Honeycutt give balance to his impetuous tendencies. London must learn humility, acceptance, and forgiveness to stay at his post.

The Gauntlet provides an honest, realistic, and somewhat autobiographical look at the struggles of a young pastor and his wife mixed with the humor of its era. The pastor faces challenges both within and without, at last acknowledging the enduring truths of his faith.

❖

Godric

Author: Frederick Buechner (1926–)

Nationality: American

Date of first publication: 1980

Approximate number of pages: 190

Available edition: HarperOne

Genres: historical novel, religious fiction, saint's life

Setting for the story: England in the twelfth century

Main characters: Godric, the protagonist who narrates the story in his own terms; Tune and Fairweather, Godric's pet snakes and close companions; Roger Mouse, Godric's fondest friend and fellow sailor; Ailred, the abbot who sends Reginald to put Godric's life in writing; Reginald, Godric's official biographer; Aedlward, his father; Aedwen, his mother; William, his brother; Burcwen, his sister with whom he has a close yet complicated relationship; Perkin, the young man who serves as the son Godric never had; Gillian, a woman who appears to Godric in several visions; Elric, the aged priest with whom he lives for several years

Plot summary: The novel is a first-person narrative recounting the life of the sinner-turned-saint Godric. While he tells his story episodically, without following a strict chronological order, his life falls roughly into two parts of equal length: his first fifty years as a sailor, merchant, and miscreant in search of worldly success, and his second fifty years as a hermit in restless pursuit of holiness. As a young man, Godric sets out in pursuit of fortune and travels the high seas with Roger Mouse, until they have a parting of ways. This propels Godric to shed his traveling name, Deric, and embrace a new course of life. Eventually, he establishes a hermitage at Finchale near the River Wear, where he lives the remainder of his days in relative isolation.

The opening sentence of the novel is one of the most arresting in all of literature: "Five friends I had, and two of them snakes." Godric tells the story of his life "from both its ends at once," supporting the novel's theme that "nothing human's not a broth of false and true, it was the two at once."

Godric has several conversion-like experiences that produce his transformation: his near drowning as a youngster, his encounter with Saint Cuthbert on the Isle of Farne, his pilgrimage to Rome and the vision he has on his return, his parting ways with Mouse and "baptism" in the River Jordan, his giving away his ill-gotten fortune as alms and meeting the aged priest Elric, and his vision of the hermitage and his own destiny.

However, Godric the saint never fully dispenses with his sin; he can part neither with the memories of who he was nor with the reality of who he still is. Hence his consistent complaint against his biographer, Reginald, whom he fears will whitewash his rather unsaintly life. This interplay delves into issues of one's true identity and the nature of saintliness.

Other issues embodied in the story include the tension between sin and grace, the ongoing struggle to mortify indwelling sin, the blessing of friendship, dealing with the remorse and guilt of wrongdoing, conversion as an event and a process, and the role of providence in shaping the course of one's life.

The God-Seeker

Author: Sinclair Lewis (1885–1951)

Nationality: American

Date of first publication: 1949

Approximate number of pages: 415

Available edition: out of print but obtainable from used-book sources and libraries

Genres: novel, historical fiction, regional writing

Settings for the story: New England and (primarily) Minnesota

Main characters: the protagonist Aaron Gadd, a frontier missionary to the Indians of Minnesota; Uriel Gadd, Aaron's fundamentalist father; Rev. Balthasar Harge, who becomes a father figure to Aaron at the Minnesota mission; Huldah, an ardent young missionary who represents the spiritual life; Selene, daughter of an Indian woman and a Scotch fur trader, representative of the earthly, native, and non-Christian

Plot Summary: Raised in Massachusetts under the rule of his father, a passionate and strict Protestant, Aaron Gadd is inspired by the evangelical preaching of Rev. Balthasar Harge to become a missionary preacher to the Sioux tribe on the Minnesota frontier. Leaving behind New England and Nadine, his romantic interest there, Gadd chooses to try to convert Native American Indians. The novel has all the usual appeals of frontier historical fiction—local geography with its rivers, lakes, and prairies; voyaging; swindlers; politicians; and religious zealots.

At one level, this book is about ministers; three of the main characters are professional clerics. Two of them represent the fundamentalist or extreme Protestant strain in American life. Aaron Gadd comes under the sway of that strain, but at the end he rejects it.

The religious importance of the novel lies in its missionary focus. The book explores in detail the many facets of cross-cultural conversion and the negative effects of American colonialism on Native American Indians. Wrestling with his conscience, Gadd asks, "Does the religion we bring them make up for the evil we bring?" The uneasy connection between well-meaning missionaries and opportunistic settlers/invaders from white society gives an Indian named Black Wolf the opportunity to denounce the influence of the Christian missionaries.

A story of both a pastoral and a missionary calling, *The God-Seeker* portrays through its characters various viewpoints on Christianity, evangelism, mission efforts, and the American frontier spirit. In the end, Gadd gives up his missionary work with the Indians, choosing instead to connect with his brother Elijah, take up with Selene, and devote himself to the Underground Railroad and labor union movement in St. Paul. This is a choice of social action over Christian conversion.

Go Tell It on the Mountain

Author: James Baldwin (1924–87)

Nationality: African American

Date of first publication: 1953

Approximate number of pages: 250

Available editions: Dell, Random House, Turtleback Books

Genres: novel, semiautobiographical novel (*Bildungsroman*), African-American narrative, coming-of-age story

Setting for the story: Harlem in New York City in the 1930s

Main characters: John Grimes, fourteen-year-old protagonist of the story who feels hated by his stepfather; Gabriel, John's pastor and supposed father (actually his stepfather); Elizabeth, John's mother; Roy, John's brother; Florence, John's aunt

Plot summary: Largely set on the fourteenth birthday of protagonist John Grimes, the story moves through the day toward John's conversion experience in the evening at the storefront Temple of the Fire Baptized Church. The novel is divided into five sections: the first focuses on the fourteen-year-old John, the second on his aunt (Florence), the third on his stepfather (Gabriel), the fourth on his mother (Elizabeth), and the fifth again on John. By means of flashbacks, the story reaches out beyond John's birthday to encompass a family's history from the rural South to the urban North.

If one takes a wide-angle view of the story, it explores issues of faith, race and racism, family, coming of age, and identity. The external action focuses on the protagonist's struggle to understand his stepfather's perceived hatred of him. The actual cause of that hatred is the father's concealed and sordid past. But this central action is nearly overwhelmed by a network of interrelated plot threads that fall into the general literary category of realism, with sex, violence, drunkenness, and death prominent features of the action. These interrelated stories fill in the background of the relationship between son and stepfather.

Viewed as a story of a minister and issues in ministry, the focus of the story falls on Gabriel, the preacher who fills the dual role of local pastor and father. As a father, Gabriel is a strict disciplinarian who is abusive to his stepson. At this level, the story is a clerical exposé. As a preacher, Gabriel preaches a message of salvation through faith in Jesus, with hell the destination of all who refuse to believe. But the gap between the message of salvation in Christ and the preacher's abusive actions toward his family make the novel an exploration of ministerial hypocrisy.

Additional features heighten the religious interest of the book. It is saturated with allusions and stylistic echoes of the King James Bible. There is also an autobiographical aspect to the story: James Baldwin himself grew up in Harlem, underwent a religious awakening at the age of fourteen, and had a stepfather who was a Pentecostal minister. One readily sees that something more than fiction is woven into the story.

Holy Masquerade

Author: Olov Hartman (1906–82)

Nationality: Swedish

Date of first publication: 1950 in Swedish; 1963 in English

Approximate number of pages: 140

Available edition: Eerdmans

Genres: novel, Lutheran fiction

Setting for the story: Sjöbo, a small country parish in Sweden

Main characters: Albert Svensson, a pastor in a rural Swedish parish; Klara, his wife

Plot summary: Klara Svensson, the agnostic wife of Albert, a hypocritical pastor, begins her diary on the Sunday before Ash Wednesday and ends it on Maundy Thursday. During her Lenten journey, she struggles with the inconsistencies and contradictions she finds in her husband's life and words as she tries to come to terms with her true identity and the meaning of their marriage. At first she seems difficult and petulant, deliberately seeing only the worst side of a pastor whose burden is an unbelieving, outspoken wife, but as she journeys deeper into Lent, the reader begins to see her growing faith and the shallowness of Albert's liberal theology. On the evening of Maundy Thursday, she discovers Albert's affair with a parishioner and perhaps inadvertently sets a fire in the church tower, during which she is badly burned. Albert picks up the narrative on Good Friday, following several police reports. He reports her subsequent death, including her deathbed conversion, which he denigrates.

The Lenten journey of confession and repentance is central to this novel. Significantly, there is no chapter for Easter Sunday (even though Albert's narrative takes us beyond the incidents of that tragic weekend), so there seems to be no room for absolution or resurrection in Albert's theology. In fact, it contains no room for the recognition of sin, especially his own. He attributes Klara's struggles to her psychological state rather than her spiritual state, even though the psychiatrist she consulted assured him that her neuroses were minor and that her questions were intensely spiritual.

Klara alludes to a masquerade several times, most obviously in connection with the charade Albert plays as he puts on a pious face while disdaining what he considers the simplistic literalism of his flock. Klara sets out to use the season of Lent to determine what her husband believes and what she herself believes. She cannot decide which of her faces is the true one—the agnostic one or the one attracted to the beliefs her husband despises. Her final words are that the masquerade has now come to an end, implying that it is difficult within this mortal life to be completely true to oneself. But these words follow her statement of belief in God and her relinquishment of her doubt.

In My Father's House

Author: Ernest J. Gaines (1933–)

Nationality: American

Date of first publication: 1978

Approximate number of pages: 215

Available edition: Vintage

Genres: novel, Southern fiction, African-American fiction, literature of the civil rights movement

Setting for the story: Louisiana in the post–Martin Luther King Jr. era

Main characters: Philip Martin, a respected minister and civil rights leader in St. Adrienne, Louisiana; Robert X, Martin's illegitimate son whose return to St. Adrienne as an adult precipitates the action; Martin's wife, Alma, a supportive wife in Martin's turbulent life during the two weeks covered in the story

Plot summary: Before Philip Martin's conversion, he led a dissolute life of gambling, sex, and drinking. All of that lies in the past. As the novel begins, Rev. Martin is a model of ministerial success—a family man, a civil rights leader in his community, affluent. Philip's life changes when his illegitimate son returns to town to kill his father. As the story unfolds, we piece together Philip's preconversion past and the consequences of his irresponsibility in regard to the mother of his three illegitimate children. Rev. Martin tries to rectify his past failings in regard to his son, but he mismanages the process in such a way that he loses his entire standing in the community and in the local civil rights movement.

Although a plot summary of this novel might convey that the book is primarily a satiric exposé of ministers, this is not quite accurate. Rev. Martin's fall from favor in his community is not, for the most part, a result of his bad actions in his ministerial role. The novel does not primarily portray ministerial failings but instead shows what happens when a person with Rev. Martin's flaws is a minister. The novel is above all a character portrayal.

A good starting point in analyzing this story is to explore the character flaws in the protagonist's life and then note how these flaws undermine his ministry and leadership in the local civil rights movement. Chief among Rev. Martin's flaws is a misguided sense of self-sufficiency. He operates as a lone wolf in his leadership roles. The story is also an exploration of how a destructive past can come back to haunt someone, especially someone in the public eye.

The novel also addresses the following issues in ministry: the effects of a bad past in a minister's life, the mismanagement that comes when a minister acts impulsively and without seeking counsel, and the negative effect on a minister's faith when his personal life unravels. In addition, the book's title serves as an interpretive framework for the novel on multiple levels.

In the Beauty of the Lilies

Author: John Updike (1932–2009)

Nationality: American

Date of first publication: 1996

Approximate number of pages: 500

Available edition: Ballantine

Genres: novel, family saga

Settings for the story: Paterson, New Jersey; a small town in Delaware; Hollywood; Colorado

Main characters: Clarence Wilmot, a Presbyterian minister who leaves the ministry when he loses his faith; Esther Wilmot, daughter of Clarence's son Teddy, who becomes a Hollywood star; Esther's son Clark (great-grandson of Clarence), who falls under the sway of a messianic preacher named Jesse Smith and enters a religious commune

Plot summary: The novel traces four generations of a ministerial family, from 1910 to 1990. Clarence is a model minister until he begins to doubt the existence of God and thereupon resigns from his pastorate and begins a career of selling encyclopedias to support his family. Clarence's resignation traumatizes his family, and son Teddy retreats to a small town in Delaware, where he embarks on the unassuming life of a mail carrier. But his daughter Esther hits the big time as a Hollywood star. In turn, her neglected son Clark leaves for Colorado and joins a religious commune, where he feels valued. The commune's charismatic, domineering pastor leads his followers to a suicidal standoff with the authorities, but Clark gets cold feet and rescues most of the women and children, though he is killed in the process.

J ohn Updike wrote multiple novels with ministers in the cast of characters, and this late work perpetuates the pattern. In the figure of Clarence Wilmot we see Updike's concern for the impact of modernism (including the media) on the ability of people to believe the supernaturalism of the Christian faith. The novel's title alludes to a famous discourse by Jesus about God's providence over his creatures (Matt. 6:19–34; Luke 12:13–34), hinting at the unifying motif of the novel: the search to find faith and consolation in the troubling realities of life. The story explores two options for constructing a coherent narrative of meaning: religion and the cinema. Neither option emerges as a convincing answer to the search for meaning.

The novel begins and ends with clerical figures. For Clarence Wilmot, being a minister means having a preoccupation with denominationalism, theological trivialities, and the politics of the elder board. His resignation from the ministry mainly means a loss of income and status for his family. He spends the rest of his life attempting to hide from his pain and fill the void created by the loss of God by escaping into the illusion of the movies. Religion comes full circle in the fourth generation of Wilmots with Clark's attraction to apocalyptic zeal, and Jesse Smith's fanaticism serves as a foil to Clarence's institutionalized Christianity. The novel explores the effects of doubt and unbelief on a pastor's life and ministry and the loneliness of ministers as they seek to nurture faith in an unreceptive culture.

The Ionian Mission

Author: Patrick O'Brian (1914–2000)

Nationality: English

Date of first publication: 1981

Approximate number of pages: 350

Available edition: Norton

Genres: naval fiction, historical fiction

Setting for the story: the world of the British Royal Navy in the age of Lord Nelson; the action takes place mainly aboard a ship at sea

Main characters: Jack Aubrey, a British post captain; Stephen Maturin, the ship's physician and British naval espionage agent; Mr. Martin, chaplain for the ship

Plot summary: Captain Aubrey is obliged to command the HMS *Worcester*, one of the most poorly built ships in the Royal Navy. Assigned to the Mediterranean fleet, his ship is given a number of missions, culminating with a political assignment that places Aubrey outside his element but ultimately concludes with the kind of desperate sea battle of which Aubrey is a former master.

Captain Jack Aubrey has never before sailed with a chaplain. But his new admiral, having evangelical leanings, desires that his ships be served by a qualified chaplain. This disturbs Aubrey, who knows that seamen consider parsons to be unlucky and who worries that a chaplain will restrict liberty of speech and camaraderie among the officers. But after Mr. Martin is assigned as chaplain to Aubrey's ship, he quickly commends himself by his eager personality, by sharing Dr. Maturin's passion for natural philosophy, and by his extraordinary felicity in conducting choir aboard ship.

Aubrey must contend with the enmity and tarnished reputation he has brought on himself through past recklessness, and his career is threatened by a poor ship and a nearly impossible mission. Aubrey must prove his valor to his followers and his all-important luck to himself. A turn of events restores him to command of his beloved frigate, HMS *Surprise*.

The title *The Ionian Mission* refers to Aubrey's mission: he must decide on a Turkish ruler to install over a valuable Ionian port. Realizing that a false move will ruin his career, Aubrey seems on the brink of a personal disaster. But at just the right moment his luck holds: one of the Turks takes to sea with his fleet, seeking to force the decision. This is just the situation Aubrey can best handle, and his success restores both his sense of luck and his reputation for bravery. As for the chaplain, Mr. Martin, he has successfully begun his naval career, having confounded the conventional superstition and brought no bad luck to the ship after all.

Jane Eyre

Author: Charlotte Brontë (1816–55)

Nationality: English

Date of first publication: 1847

Approximate number of pages: 500

Available editions: numerous editions

Genres: novel, coming-of-age story, gothic literature

Setting for the story: middle and north England from 1810 to 1840

Main characters: Jane Eyre (the narrator), a young woman without family; Edward Rochester, a brusque, worldly, and mysterious man

Plot summary: Told in the first person, the story follows Jane from an orphan shunned by wealthy relatives, to a student at a bleak charity school, to a governess in a mysterious house. Finding unlikely companionship and love with her employer, Edward Rochester, Jane is forced to leave him when a secret from his past is revealed. She finds refuge with a clergyman and his sisters, yet still she is faced with the challenges of calling and principle.

From the book's outset, Jane Eyre is a character torn by the calls of sympathy and principle. As a love-starved orphan living off the charity of others, Jane is given strict training with regard to duty and morality. Yet this training is tainted, administered hypocritically and with a severity bordering on abuse. Formidable and exacting toward her, yet given to self-indulgence and favoritism, Jane's aunt Reed and the cleric Mr. Brocklehurst come to represent all that is antithetical to Jane's own character. Thus the friendless young Jane becomes principled and self-reliant, traits that serve her well throughout the story.

Themes of pastoral sympathy and principle are particularly relevant in the story of St. John Rivers, the young clergyman who with his sisters takes Jane in after she has left Edward. St. John is a principled and disciplined man, but dispassionate. Unlike other clerics in the novel, St. John is genuine in his integrity and zealous in his faith. Having cut off all emotion, however, he is unable to minister wholly to those closest to him. Ironically, Jane takes on a ministerial role, urging him to sympathy and love. But when he proposes that Jane marry him and join him on the mission field, it is not out of love for her nor for the people to whom he will minister. While recognizing the worth of his calling, Jane resists a marriage without love, and St. John must leave to minister to foreign peoples alone.

By the story's end, Jane and Edward are reunited, and the final chapter of the book briefly depicts their marriage and closes with a letter from St. John on the mission field. While the disparity of the two situations is obvious, the author brings them together in parallel. Whereas St. John has been far more successful ministering in foreign lands than on his native soil, Jane and Edward minister to one another in affection and love. Both are commended in their callings.

◆◆◆

Jonah's Gourd Vine

Author: Zora Neale Hurston (1891–1960)

Nationality: American

Date of first publication: 1934

Approximate number of pages: 300

Available edition: Harper

Genres: novel, domestic fiction, regional writing

Setting for the story: Eatonville, Florida, the nation's first incorporated African-American township, in the postwar South

Main characters: John Buddy Pearson, a fiery, philandering pastor; Lucy, his long-suffering wife

Plot summary: John Buddy's life is defined by both his ambition and his weakness as he rises and falls in the African-American community.

Self-control does not seem to be part of John Buddy Pearson's character. He reflexively breaks promises, from an unimportant pledge to his mother not to wade in the creek to a holy vow to his wife, Lucy, to be faithful to their marriage. His default action is self-indulgence, yet he is a hard worker, and determination has taken him far in life. John Buddy makes his way up from a shack beside a cotton field to be the respected pastor of Zion Hope and mayor of Eatonville, Florida, an all-black town. Lucy, whom he has desired since she was twelve, is his wife, and the fruits of family, ministry, and community should be enough to satisfy him.

But his string of extramarital affairs endangers the happy life he has with Lucy and the unity of his congregation, though neither of these risks compel John Buddy to stop taking what he wants. He lives voraciously, devouring words when he learns to read and write as a teenager, delivering sermons more passionately than any other area pastor, and taking women to his bed as they appeal. John loves his wife and his church, yet he damages both. Though he rarely seems to resist temptation, he inspires sympathy, and those who love him mourn his unwillingness to curb his appetites.

When Lucy's death removes her protection and unflagging support, John Buddy is lost. His next wife turns to "hoodoo" to keep him faithful. When this inefficient dark magic is revealed, the family and the church are finally torn apart. Now John Buddy's determination and giftedness are not enough to save him. Bereft of his position and the admiration of his community, John Buddy struggles until a kind widow takes pity on him. Once again John has the opportunity to do the right thing by a good wife.

John Buddy Pearson is a vibrant, flawed minister who disregards the people and personal giftedness that have aided him in his meteoric rise. When those shields are removed, he is left exposed and fragile.

◆ ◆ ◆

Les Misérables

Author: Victor Hugo (1802–85)

Nationality: French

Date of first publication: 1862

Approximate number of pages: 1,200

Available editions: numerous editions

Genres: novel, historical fiction, romantic fiction, satire

Settings for the story: Paris and various French towns from 1815 to 1833

Main characters: Jean Valjean, a reformed ex-convict; his adopted daughter, Cosette; Javert, a police officer pursuing Valjean

Plot summary: The novel follows the post-conversion life of ex-convict Jean Valjean as he strives to live virtuously while avoiding recapture for having broken parole. *Les Misérables* weaves together stories of thieves, revolutionaries, suffering children, the impoverished working class, students, and soldiers to celebrate nineteenth-century France, denounce its injustices, and proclaim its glorious future.

Les Misérables opens with an extended positive description of a clerical figure. A series of anecdotes highlights the piety, humility, and generosity of the bishop of Digne, who lives in near poverty in order to give liberally to the needy of his see. It is no surprise, then, that he offers hospitality to the disillusioned and brutish outcast Valjean, a recently released prisoner. When Valjean repays his goodness with burglary, the bishop forgives him, an act that forms the foundation of Valjean's conversion. The bishop of Digne virtually disappears after the first hundred pages of the novel, but his influence is felt throughout the book in Valjean's newfound philanthropy and integrity.

Valjean's later life testifies to the transformative power of forgiveness and love. As the story unfolds, he takes on the noble qualities of the bishop. He lives simply, loves wholeheartedly, gives generously, and demonstrates willingness to sacrifice his life for others. While the holy life seems relatively effortless for the bishop, Valjean experiences moral challenges that test his character. Though he struggles inwardly, he chooses integrity over expediency. By the novel's end, he has developed into a model disciple changed by forgiveness and a Christlike figure.

Serving as a foil to Valjean is the police agent Javert, whose sense of morality and duty includes no notion of forgiveness. He believes in the letter of the law to the point of cruelty, and his dogged pursuit of Valjean creates dramatic and moral suspense for the story. When he, too, experiences undeserved forgiveness, Javert psychologically and spiritually collapses.

Valjean's transformation takes place against the background of a society in need of transformation. While criticizing injustice, Victor Hugo expresses unwavering belief that an enlightened and just society will soon emerge. The novel affirms the value of mercy, the beauty of generosity, and the power of a transformed life, all set in motion by an act of forgiveness.

Light from Heaven

Author: Jan Karon (1937–)

Nationality: American

Date of first publication: 2005

Approximate number of pages: 400

Available editions: Penguin, Viking

Genres: novel, regional or local-color writing, domestic fiction

Setting for the story: the area around Mitford, a small North Carolina mountain town

Main characters: Father Timothy Kavanaugh, a retired Episcopal priest; Agnes Merton, a caretaker for a deserted church and an Episcopal deaconess

Plot summary: Though officially retired, Father Tim is spending the year fully involved in reclamation projects. He works to restart a mountain church, supposedly abandoned for forty years. With his wife, he also takes in a mistreated fifteen-year-old boy with a family connection. As illustrated by the characters' lives, the book's main theme is a reminder to hope in God's provision with perseverance, patience, and expectation.

In his first year of retirement, Father Tim is anxious to learn about a project at which his bishop has hinted. Despite their best intentions to accomplish nothing more than to read and perfect a recipe for oven fries during their year-long house-sitting stay at a nearby farm, Father Tim and his wife, Cynthia, both take on projects that were most definitely not on their agenda. While Cynthia, a children's author and illustrator, is inspired to paint farm scenes amid the disruption of farmhouse repairs, Father Tim is asked to restart tiny Holy Trinity, a church reportedly abandoned for forty years. When he visits the country parish, however, he finds that the church has been lovingly cared for by Agnes Merton and her son, who have been faithfully praying that God would send them a vicar to minister to the isolated mountain inhabitants.

In addition to serving the new flock and restarting church services, the Kavanaughs attempt another kind of restoration: they take in Sammy Barlowe, the fifteen-year-old brother of Dooley, whom the Kavanaughs have cared for since he showed up on their doorstep ten years earlier. When he leaves his abusive father, Sammy faces the choice to strike out on his own or live with the restrictions that come with the benefits of a loving family. As one Barlowe child becomes an official Kavanaugh, the search continues for one remaining missing brother.

As she and Father Tim visit those living around the church, Agnes shares what brought her to the mountain and what caused her to return, confident that God would bring what was needed. Father Tim, as worried and faith-filled as ever, remains the heart of this story, strongly emphasizing the importance of connection with friends and family, both old and new.

⟨◆—◆—◆⟩

The Mackerel Plaza

Author: Peter DeVries (1910–93)

Nationality: American

Date of first publication: 1958

Approximate number of pages: 300

Available edition: Penguin

Genres: novel, dark comedy, local-color writing, love story

Setting for the story: the northeastern suburb of Avalon, Connecticut, in the 1950s

Main characters: Rev. Andrew Mackerel, pastor of the People's Liberal Church, recent widower, and narrator; Frank Turnbull, a born-again Christian and parishioner; Molly Calico, a young administrative assistant; Hester Pedlock, Mackerel's sister-in-law and caretaker of the parsonage

Plot summary: The novel tells the comic story of Rev. Andrew Mackerel's conversion from intellectual liberalism to a belief in God, while depicting changing worldly values. His once-popular brand of freethinking liberalism is losing ground to a resurgent evangelical Christianity; this deterioration of liberalism is highlighted by Mackerel's own personal collapse, brought about by his narcissism.

Rev. Andrew Mackerel begins the story believing himself to be the portrait of what a modern clergyman should be. He fancies himself an intellectual, quotes thinkers like Freud and Auden, and intently wishes for his congregants to be as enlightened as he is. He does, however, possess a comically inflated sense of self, occasionally breaking into third-person narration to make his life seem more noteworthy. His diehard atheism and intolerance of evangelical Christianity also prove to be a major problem.

Amid Mackerel's personal decline, the novel addresses his obstinate rejection of traditional religion. As his devotion to modern philosophical enlightenment grows stronger and his defenses of it become ironically more hostile, the town of Avalon gradually returns to the traditional faith, much to Mackerel's chagrin. As he implores his fellow townsfolk to open their eyes to the truth, he schemes and lies, initially to keep his budding romance with Molly Calico a secret.

As his schemes and plots come to tragic ends, his relationships with the people of Avalon suffer, until he finally becomes a suspect in a murder case. In Mackerel's decline, Peter DeVries crafts a critique of the diehard reaction to fundamentalism. Mackerel's uncompromising spirit and unwillingness to consider why people might need faith turn him into a comically hypocritical character who is doomed to fail. Despite Mackerel's shortcomings, the objects of his attacks are not spared either. Often falling victim to DeVries's quick wit, but occasionally to their own foibles, those moving back toward evangelical Christianity cannot be called normative. Instead, the ideal seems to be a middle ground between the two positions, summed up in Mackerel's humble admission that there must at least be an intelligent designer of the universe.

A Man for All Seasons

Author: Robert Bolt (1924–95)

Nationality: English

Date of first publication: 1960

Approximate number of pages: 160

Available edition: Vintage

Genres: drama, martyr's life, saint's life, historical fiction

Settings for the story: various London settings (Thomas More's home in Chelsea, Hampton Court, Tower of London), 1529–35

Main characters: Thomas More, a hero of conscience; King Henry VIII, who assembles a nucleus of allies to pressure Thomas More to agree to his divorce and remarriage

Plot summary: The story material comes straight from English history. King Henry VIII of England needed a male heir to perpetuate the Tudor monarchy. His first wife produced no living male child, so Henry unsuccessfully requested that the pope annul the marriage. Henry divorced his first wife and remarried anyway. Parliament passed the Act of Supremacy, whereby citizens declared loyalty to the king. Thomas More, a staunch Catholic, refused to sign the act. Henry was determined to rid himself of this silent opponent and eventually engineered his beheading, which constitutes the final event in the story.

The heroic character of Thomas More dominates the play. His courage in refusing to disobey his conscience embodies the play's main message.

Thus, any reflection on or discussion of the play will necessarily explore the ways in which a minister or parishioner would wish to emulate the saintly protagonist of the play.

Although this play routinely makes it onto lists of literary portrayals of clerics, we need to set the record straight: Thomas More received some theological education; he entertained the possibility of entering the priesthood before choosing to be a lawyer; in the play, Cardinal Wolsey tells him, "You should have been a cleric"; but the fact is that Thomas More was not a cleric. The two priests in the play are minor characters. Cardinal Wolsey appears early and is a pawn of the king, attempting to bully More to acquiesce to the king's desires. Archbishop Thomas Cranmer appears late in the play as a bureaucratic representative of the church who oversees the technicalities of More's trial.

The issues the play raises about ministry focus on the potential for ministers to be weak and unprincipled before the threats of tyrannical power and to betray the gospel and the true church in that weakness. Of course, the triumph of the play is the triumph of Thomas More's own life: it is the story of the courage to remain true to one's Christian conscience even to the point of martyrdom.

Mansfield Park

Author: Jane Austen (1775–1817)

Nationality: English

Date of first publication: 1814

Approximate number of pages: 350

Available editions: numerous editions

Genres: novel, coming-of-age story, romance, morality story

Setting for the story: Mansfield Park, a fictional estate in Northamptonshire, England, in the nineteenth-century romantic era

Main characters: Fanny Price, niece and ward of Sir Thomas Bertram, master of Mansfield Park; Edmund Bertram, Sir Thomas's son studying to be a clergyman; Henry and Mary Crawford, siblings of the local rector's wife

Plot summary: The main story occurs in the space of two years in which the teenage Fanny is witness to the unfolding drama involving the other inhabitants of Mansfield Park and the surrounding estate.

Because Fanny Price and Edmund Bertram are more conservative, somber, and thoughtful than the other young inhabitants of Mansfield, their decisions often put them at odds with their friends and relations. Edmund's decision to become a clergyman is no exception. At a time when it is more acceptable to be in the military or politics, he often must defend his decision to individuals within and without his family.

Edmund is an aspiring pastor in an age when the clergy is declining in social prominence. In addition, conservative, patriarchal country living as encapsulated by Mansfield Park is declining in the face of metropolitan, secularist society. Thus, Edmund is challenged to prove his worth to a society that does not want him. Dialogues about religion throughout the novel draw distinct lines between characters in the old and new schools of thought. While Sir Thomas, Edmund, and Fanny frequently advocate a minister's consistent involvement in the everyday life of his parish as crucial to the maintenance of stable society, the Crawfords clearly see church as a weekly diversion from their social calendar. To Mary in particular, clergymen are idle, selfish, bungling, hypocritical, embarrassing, and unwanted, a stereotype Edmund tries to counter even as other clerical figures in the story affirm it.

The casting of a clergyman as the hero and a meek, modest young woman as the heroine is important to the framework of social conservatism Jane Austen created for this novel. The clash of conservatism personified by Fanny and Edmund and secularism in the form of Henry and Mary creates tension throughout the novel. Ultimately, Fanny and Edmund suit each other not because of initial attraction but because of their similarity of mind and values. As the moral core of Austen's novel, their union represents the triumph of social, spiritual, and moral conservatism.

◈—◈—◈

March

Author: Geraldine Brooks (1955–)

Nationality: Australian

Date of first publication: 2005

Approximate number of pages: 275

Available edition: Viking

Genres: novel, historical fiction, domestic fiction

Settings for the story: Civil War–era battlefields, plantations, and a military hospital; Concord, Massachusetts

Main character: Mr. March, a Union Army chaplain

Plot summary: Mr. March, the absent father in Louisa May Alcott's *Little Women*, recounts what shaped his abolitionist convictions, what happened during his tenure as a chaplain and teacher during the Civil War, and how his marriage and his self-respect are tested by the events that unfold during the war.

Geraldine Brooks imagines the life of Mr. March, the letter-writing father gone to war as chaplain in Louisa May Alcott's *Little Women*. Through his narration, March reveals himself to be a complicated man: idealistic, naive, strongly committed to moral behavior yet heartbreakingly weak at crucial moments, in turns self-aggrandizing and self-reproaching at exactly the wrong times, with a tendency to misread people and their motives.

March is so committed to abolition that he bankrupts his family in support of the cause and impetuously volunteers to serve the Union Army as a chaplain despite his advanced age.

In letters home to Marmee and their four daughters, March avoids recounting his reunion with Grace, an educated, beautiful slave whom he had come to care for years ago while touring the South as a young peddler. Witnessing her brutal punishment had solidified his growing commitment to abolition.

When March is unexpectedly reunited with Grace at a battlefield hospital, a momentary show of his deep emotions for her prompts his reassignment to a plantation liberated from Southern ownership. There March finds success teaching the "contraband" freed slaves while cajoling the Northerner now working the cotton fields to improve the quality of life for those who have chosen to stay.

When the tide of the war turns unexpectedly, former slaves fighting for the Confederates overrun the land, killing some and taking others hostage, including March. March survives and is sent north to a military hospital, where he once again finds Grace, who is now working as a nurse. As the physical state of March deteriorates, Marmee comes to tend to him. As she begins to understand the attraction between her husband and Grace, Marmee questions whether she truly knows March and whether she is willing to have him rejoin their family. Forgiving oneself and others for both real and perceived wrongs is at the heart of this story of a tender man scarred by war.

Men and Brethren

Author: James Gould Cozzens (1903–78)

Nationality: American

Date of first publication: 1936

Approximate number of pages: 200

Available edition: Ivan R. Dee

Genres: novel, regional or local-color writing

Setting for the story: New York City in the 1920s

Main character: Rev. Ernest Cudlipp, vicar of St. Ambrose

Plot summary: The story relays the events that occur during a weekend in the life of Rev. Ernest Cudlipp, an Episcopal priest in New York City. Over the course of the weekend, Cudlipp encounters numerous friends, colleagues, and parishioners all in need of his guidance as they deal with major crises in their lives. Even as he counsels others, Cudlipp undergoes his own crisis of faith.

Rev. Ernest Cudlipp is the vicar of St. Ambrose Episcopal Chapel in New York City. His early years serving in the church were spent in a liberal congregation in which carnal passion was condoned and profane essays were read from the pulpit in place of sermons. Now a confirmed celibate bachelor in his mid-forties, his doctrine has shifted to the conservative, though his methods of engaging people remain rather unorthodox. Cudlipp is a pragmatist who uses his insight into those around him to tailor his approach to their current situation, background, and beliefs.

The main action of the novel is Cudlipp's internal struggle for purpose in his life. This struggle is provoked, highlighted, and ultimately resolved through his interaction with his friends and parishioners. Over the course of a weekend, he interacts with numerous people who need his assistance and guidance. These encounters include poets, housewives, and fellow priests, all of whom are dealing with quintessential life crises. One is pregnant through an adulterous encounter, another is fleeing his father to marry his love, while another is a fellow priest caught in homosexuality. As the vicar is confronted with these situations and the questions they raise, he starts to examine his own life and questions his true motivation for remaining vicar. He questions whether he remains in the position out of convenience or pride and begins to contemplate retirement.

Ultimately, by helping others work through their crises, Cudlipp realizes that everyone has been called to certain responsibilities based on the gifts they have been given. He comes to a greater realization of God's hand in guiding even the smallest aspects of life. In light of these revelations, he accepts that through all the events in his life he has been gifted, prepared, and called to be vicar. The novel ends as Cudlipp contemplates the parable of the talents and reaffirms his commitment to his position in the church.

◆──◆──◆

The Minister's Wooing

Author: Harriet Beecher Stowe (1811–96)

Nationality: American

Date of first publication: 1859

Approximate number of pages: 385

Available edition: Penguin

Genres: fiction, romance

Setting for the story: Newport, Rhode Island, in eighteenth-century Puritan New England

Main characters: Dr. Samuel Hopkins, town minister; Catherine and Mary Scudder, hosts of Dr. Hopkins; Aaron Burr, infamous son of Jonathan Edwards; James Marvyn, young man in love with Mary

Plot summary: The story follows God's wooing of a noble-minded though ineffective minister to himself by working in him an act of such sweet sacrifice in personal romance that it elevates not only the minister but also his people to a deeper experience of the high call of God's Word and grace.

This is a story that separates the dross from the gold in Puritan theology and instills a grand vision of God's goodness. Dr. Samuel Hopkins, the town minister, though a Puritan, is a pioneer of a new theology as he splits hairs over the finer points of Calvinism. The women of the congregation are enthralled and captivated by his sermons, while most men are bored.

The story is also one of contrasts. Dr. Hopkins, while boring in the pulpit, is committed to self-denial and sacrifice for God's will and the sake of the people. This is set over against the figure of Aaron Burr: self-indulgent, unscrupulous, and without self-control in his lust for power and women. Young Mary is a Puritan in the best sense of the word—a lover of God who longs to please him. She is well trained in self-denial and wary of worldly pleasures. She is also in love with a childhood friend (James Marvyn) who finds Dr. Hopkins's sermons irrelevant to his life. Because of Mary's devotion, she is unable to commit herself to James since he is not a believer. He sails away on the sea.

157

When Mary recovers from this trauma, Dr. Hopkins begins to woo her. Eventually, she agrees to his proposal of marriage, and he is overcome by God's goodness to an aging and unworthy bachelor. On the eve of their wedding, James reappears. He has become a true believer and presents himself to Mary as now worthy of her love. Mary refuses to break her engagement to Dr. Hopkins because of her commitment to duty.

When Dr. Hopkins is told of the conflict, he spends a night in agony of soul, wrestling with God's goodness in taking from him the greatest joy he has ever known. His decision to release Mary from the engagement brings an end to the minister's wooing, which has really been God's wooing of him ever upward to himself. Thus, the greatest achievement of grace in the lives of his congregants happens not through the theology he preaches but through this sorrow suffered and sacrifice acted out before them.

<hr>

Moby-Dick

Author: Herman Melville (1819–91)

Nationality: American

Date of first publication: 1851

Approximate number of pages: 650

Available editions: numerous editions

Genres: novel, psychological fiction, sea story, adventure story

Setting for the story: a nineteenth-century whaling ship, the *Pequod*

Main characters: Ishmael, the narrator of the story and a ship hand on the ship named the *Pequod*; Ahab, captain of the *Pequod;* Moby Dick, the white whale that Ahab obsessively chases

Plot summary: Ishmael tells the story of the whaling ship *Pequod* during its unrelenting pursuit of Moby Dick. The story begins when Ishmael, the philosophically inclined narrator, enlists in a whaling voyage, hoping to gain understanding about the world through his time at sea. The goal of the crew's quest is to kill a vicious sperm whale known as Moby Dick. This gigantic beast has severed one of Ahab's legs and killed other whalers in its attempts to escape their harpoons. In Ahab's obsessed mind, the malignant creature is an embodiment of evil. After a months-long voyage, the crew finds Moby Dick and engages him in a three-day battle. Eventually, the whale destroys the ship and all its crew members except the narrator.

The cleric in the story is Father Mapple, minister at New Bedford's Whaling Chapel. His ministry is to itinerants (people passing through) and to mariners in a seaport town. His small congregation is a collection of fearful, excited whalers about to embark, anxious wives awaiting their seamen, and the grief-stricken widows of those dead or missing at sea. Once a harpooner himself, Father Mapple understands the emotions of the men and women facing an uncertain future. In the famous sermon recounted in the novel, Father Mapple tells the story of Jonah. Perhaps because he knows he will never see many of the listeners again, Father Mapple emphasizes one point: to obey God, one must disobey one's very nature. He wants his listeners to understand that they sin, struggling against the truth to embrace a falsehood. As Jonah found, the only surety in life is to entrust oneself to God and his plans.

In this brief masterpiece of local-color writing, Ishmael finds comfort in Father Mapple's words and in the little chapel itself. The pulpit is shaped like the prow of a ship. It makes sense to Ishmael that the place from which the Bible is taught would be like the first part of a ship to encounter the sea, reinforcing the Bible's strength and its fight against darkness. Though Ishmael spends only a short time at the chapel preparing for his voyage, what he hears prepares him for his journey with Captain Ahab.

◆―◆―◆

A Month of Sundays

Author: John Updike (1932–2009)

Nationality: American

Date of first publication: 1974

Approximate number of pages: 230

Available edition: Penguin

Genres: novel, journal

Settings for the story: a town in the Midwest; a desert retreat center in the southwestern United States

Main characters: Rev. Tom Marshfield; Ms. Prynne, his caretaker

Plot summary: After a series of affairs with women in his congregation, Rev. Tom Marshfield is sent off by his bishop (Ned Bork) for a month of reflection, recuperation, poker, and golf. Ms. Prynne, the caretaker who oversees Marshfield's recuperation, suggests that he keep a daily journal as a form of therapy. The novel consists of the resulting thirty-one journal entries. In his writings, Marshfield details the events that led to his month away: a failing faith, a troubled marriage, and most significantly, an all-consuming, ravenous sexual appetite. Yet even as he reflects on his extramarital relations and ever-weakening faith, he cannot resist cunningly seducing and finally sleeping with Ms. Prynne.

It is clear from the start that Tom Marshfield is not a typical Christian preacher. He is cynical, crude, blasphemous, and the victim of what appears to be an uncontrollable sexual obsession. On the surface he looks to be nothing more than a blasphemous preacher with a dirty mouth and mind to match his reprehensible actions. But at the same time, he is also an observant, thoughtful character. Although sometimes he appears to renounce God and Christianity, his thoughts as a whole reflect more of a struggle in faith than a stubborn atheism.

The theme of his life as a minister seems to be best reflected not by his early comment that he is "finally free" of Christianity but by his honest statement, "I have no faith. Or, rather, I have faith but it doesn't seem to apply." Beneath his candid, crude, cutting commentary, Marshfield seems to honestly struggle to reconcile the faith he professes with the earthly world he experiences. Primarily, his inability to overcome powerful sexual urges causes him to conclude that the faith he preaches must be inapplicable or foolish or both. Perhaps the best articulations of this struggle are the four sermons he writes during his month of rehabilitation. These sermons, though for the most part completely blasphemous, raise some important issues that all Christians must address, such as the problem of suffering.

Rev. Marshfield provides a poignant example of a preacher's sin and personal struggle with faith. Beneath the vulgar sexual overtones and blasphemous cynicism, Marshfield is a thought-provoking example of how faith can go awry, even in the life of a minister.

Morte d'Urban

Author: J. F. Powers (1917–99)

Nationality: American

Date of first publication: 1962

Approximate number of pages: 340

Available edition: New York Review Books

Genres: novel, comedy

Setting for the story: rural Minnesota in the 1960s

Main characters: Father Urban, a Roman Catholic priest; Billy Cosgrove, a businessman; Father Boniface, a rival priest

Plot summary: Father Urban, an up-and-coming charismatic priest, attracts jealousy from other priests and is sent to a backwoods Minnesota retreat center, away from the political action in his order. Although sidestepped in this way, his ambition does not wane.

Father Urban is convinced that he is a first-rate priest wasted in the third-rate Order of St. Clement. He was given the assignment of traveling the country to give speeches for the Catholic Church. Father Urban's speeches were flamboyant and drew attention to himself. Though he was faithful to his vows of poverty, he loved to move among the wealthy. He was full of ideas for advancing the prominence of the order, eager to fill it with unconventional, exciting priests like the one who attracted him to the religious life. To fund these ideas, Father Urban turns to Chicago businessman Billy Cosgrove, a generous but innately cruel man. When Father Boniface, the head of the district, senses that Father Urban is a rival for his job, he reassigns him to rural, heavily Protestant Minnesota to turn a dilapidated building into a retreat center.

Resentful but obedient, Father Urban relocates to the small town of Deusterhaus, Minnesota, to undertake the renovations. Father Urban begins a passive war to get back to life as a functioning priest, where he can serve faithfully and, happily, be admired at the same time. After a year, Urban briefly escapes the retreat center when he is appointed to replace a vacationing priest at St. Monica's, a parish in a nearby town. Though there only six weeks, Father Urban reenergizes the parish and himself and is once again full of ideas and eager to accomplish great things.

When he returns to the center, Father Urban intends to attract the "right sort" of person (wealthy and not necessarily Catholic) to stay at the retreat. He schemes to have his donor, Billy, buy the land next to the center to turn it into a golf course, which becomes a booming success. It is also the scene of a physical injury that puts Father Urban on a collision course with his own frailties and the morally suspect donors he has cultivated. When he is given a longed-for appointment within the order, it becomes apparent that his time in exile has changed his temperament and his convictions.

Old Mortality

Author: Sir Walter Scott (1771–1832)

Nationality: Scottish

Date of first publication: 1816 as *Tales of Old Mortality*

Approximate number of pages: 545

Available edition: Penguin

Genre: historical novel

Setting for the story: seventeenth-century southwest Scotland

Main characters: Henry Morton of Milnwood, a moderate Presbyterian; John Balfour of Burley, one of the assassins of Archbishop James Sharp; Cuddie Headrigg, a peasant; ministers Macbriar, Poundtext, and Kettledrum

Plot summary: The bulk of the novel surrounds the military campaign waged by John Graham of Claverhouse's government forces against a Covenanting army. The hero, Henry Morton, is arrested by Claverhouse's troops for harboring John Balfour of Burley, a Covenanting friend of his father, without knowledge that he had participated in the murder of Archbishop Sharp. The archbishop was hated by the Covenanters aiding the restoration of Episcopalianism, the event that triggered the uprising. Morton is sentenced to death but is eventually saved through the intervention of Lord Evandale, his friend and rival for the hand of Edith Bellenden.

The three Covenanter ministers in this novel do not stand up well. Poundtext is the weak moderate. Sound in doctrine, he advocates peaceful coexistence with the Anglican English. But he is not a leader and cannot stand against stronger opposition. Kettledrum is an old fundamentalist who speaks boldly against any concession with the English, but only when at a safe distance. In truth, he is a coward. The daring minister is the young Macbriar, a fiery zealot who can bear no deviation from the pure Covenanting religion and who blindly leads his forces to their destruction.

Sir Walter Scott probes the dangers of both religious fanaticism, as exhibited by the Covenanters, and the intolerance of the state against religious conviction, as exhibited by the English occupiers. Both extremes lead otherwise reasonable people to destructive actions. The "pure" of heart Covenanter leaders and ministers, in their zeal to establish God's kingdom in Scotland, reveal the same sins of ambition and malicious hatred that they ascribe to their English oppressors. The minister who has zeal without knowledge (or, rather, without gospel love) causes not only his own demise but also the destruction of his sheep who trustingly follow him, in this case the Covenanter army.

The book adds a voice to today's debate about the role of religion in the social and political arena. It allows us to see the relationship between the kingdom of God and the kingdom of man played out in another age.

One Foot in Heaven:
The Life of a Practical Parson

Author: Hartzell Spence (1908–2001)

Nationality: American

Date of first publication: 1940

Approximate number of pages: 300

Available edition: out of print but obtainable from used-book sources and libraries

Genres: biographical narrative (creative nonfiction), local-color writing

Settings for the story: rural and small-town Iowa; Omaha, Nebraska; Denver, Colorado; 1910–35

Main characters: William H. Spence, faithful pastor of a variety of Methodist churches; his wife, Hope, who provides wisdom and grace; his children, Eileen, Hartzell (author of the book), and Fraser

Plot summary: The story recounts the everyday life and work of a Methodist minister who adapts wisely to life without losing his belief in the need for conversion and dedicated Christian living. Though he respects his father's convictions, the author strongly hints that his father needed to change his doctrine, not just his methods, to fit the times.

The book begins and ends with examples of what the author considers his father's practical Christianity. The opening chapter recounts the pastor's preaching about new birth in Christ on Palm Sunday. Interrupted by a report that the parsonage is on fire, he closes the service quickly rather than continuing per tradition. The closing chapter describes the old pastor, now suffering from debilitating heart disease and waiting to die, certain that though the old Methodist ways are gone, the people's hearts remain true.

The intervening chapters contribute to the portrayal of Spence's integrity and humanity. His integrity shines when he leaves medical school to serve in a rural parish. It is evident when he helps hurting people and rebukes self-seeking church leaders. It is most obvious when he protects the author from a malicious personal attack. His humanity reveals itself mainly in his relationships with his wife—with whom he has several gentle disagreements—and his children, for whom he must adapt to their need to be young people, not simply pastor's kids. This humanity also appears in descriptions of his ambition, restlessness, and occasional thoughtless legalistic behavior. It is most touching in the final scene, where he expresses pride in his son, the author.

This book stresses that although times and people change, certain qualities of a minister should be timeless. Regardless of the passing of time, William H.

Spence never rejects the need to stress salvation from sin, Christian charity, and practical Christian living. He always deals with people as people, not objects. From these and other core beliefs he forges a ministry marked by wisdom in crisis.

<hr>

The Poisonwood Bible

Author: Barbara Kingsolver (1958–)

Nationality: American

Date of first publication: 1998

Approximate number of pages: 540

Available edition: HarperCollins

Genres: novel, travel story, missionary story

Settings for the story: begins in Georgia in the 1950s and then moves to a missionary setting in the Congo

Main characters: Rev. Nathan and Mrs. Price and their four daughters: Ruth, Leah, Adah, and Rachel

Plot summary: The lives of the four observant Price girls are changed by their father's intractable mission to Africa as the Congo fought for its independence. This novel is a poignant account of how the family survives in Africa amid the unstable circumstances, and it gives readers an inside look into how faith and conviction can change people. This encyclopedic book is divided into separate chapters labeled "books," and each of these is named after a female family member. The result is that we see the blunders and controlling actions of the pastor from the varied and unique perspectives of his wife and daughters.

"Man's inhumanity to man" is generally considered a terrible indictment of the cruel human suffering imposed by one human upon other humans. But the phrase might also be used to describe noble purposes gone so tragically awry that expected cultural adeptness, civility, and respect elicit intolerable ignorance, rage, and bitterness, resulting in appalling social and spiritual disconnect. In a nutshell, this is the calamitous missionary endeavor of a fundamentalist Baptist evangelist who takes his wife and four young daughters from Georgia to the Belgian Congo to preach his convoluted brand of Christianity to the heathen. The portrayal of the evangelist father is largely negative.

The story is told insightfully by Nathan's wife and four daughters. All see Africa through a different lens. The girls are self-centered and shrewd and possess prophetic foresight. The mother is darkened by her own losses. The father is busy fighting his own unrecognized, unacknowledged demons. This American family is incapable of recognizing that the Congolese were perceptive beyond belief, and if one only took the time and effort to study them, one would find them polite, something the Price family cannot see.

Sometimes the stereotype of the zealot lacking knowledge is far too caricatured, but not in this story, where the inflexible Rev. Price is so occupied with mistaken issues that he could repeatedly shout at the end of his Sunday sermons, "Jesus is bangala." *Bangala* pronounced a certain way means something precious and dear, while pronounced another way (the subtlety unnoticed by Rev. Price) means poisonwood, a noxious weed causing terrible, unrelieved itching.

A Portrait of the Artist as a Young Man

Author: James Joyce (1882–1941)

Nationality: Irish

Date of first publication: 1914

Approximate number of pages: 320

Available editions: numerous editions

Genre: semiautobiographical novel (*Bildungsroman*)

Setting for the story: a Jesuit chapel school in Dublin, Ireland, in the early 1900s; a time of political unrest and deep Roman Catholic religious devotion

Main characters: Stephen Dedalus, the protagonist; Father Arnall, a priest; Cranly, Stephen's closest and most irreligious friend at the university

Plot summary: This story is built around the theme of independence for the sake of artistry. The narrative portrays a young student who grows out of Irish politics and religion in order to grow into an artist. Living in a time when Irish nationality and the Catholic faith were binding moral forces in Ireland's social conscience, Stephen frees himself to develop a love for words and a passion for the artistry of poetry, all built upon the foundation of the old god of Rome and the new god of nationalism. As the protagonist matures in his literary capabilities and artistry, the artistic evolution of the society is also indirectly reflected.

This is a deeply theological novel. A good portion of the text is devoted to Father Arnall's three fiery sermons on hell. These sermons, preached over the course of a three-day retreat, form the center of this novel. Before the retreat, Stephen had been living in a state of "mortal sin," having had relations with a number of prostitutes. With each sermon, Stephen develops an increasing fear of death and hell. Compelled to change, he confesses his sins to Father Arnall, thus beginning a new life of complete devotion to the Catholic faith. Yet even with his asceticism—his self-abasement of each of his five bodily senses—as well as his toying with the idea of entering the religious life, he finds the practices and goals of holiness to be, in Paul's words, of "no value against fleshly indulgence" (Col. 2:23). He then returns to "the insistent voices of the flesh," giving in to his previous temptations and vices.

It is not until he hears another voice, one calling him to embrace sensual beauty as the epitome of goodness and truth, that he finally frees himself from shame and guilt and flees into the heights of his true life calling—to be a writer. The final chapters find the protagonist at the university, no longer fighting his fleshly temptations to sin, nor fighting for his country out of nationalism, but instead striving to find and express his true self through the artistry of words. In studying this novel, readers can explore the reasons for Father Arnall's failure to connect with the schoolboys and influence Stephen Dedalus to embrace Christianity.

⬥⬥⬥

Pride and Prejudice

Author: Jane Austen (1775–1817)

Nationality: English

Date of first publication: 1813

Approximate number of pages: 375

Available editions: numerous editions

Genres: domestic fiction, comedy of manners

Setting for the story: nineteenth-century English countryside

Main characters: Elizabeth Bennet, protagonist and one of five sisters in quest for a husband; Fitzwilliam Darcy, conceited suitor; Rev. William Collins, the minister in the story

Plot summary: Attempts to match five sisters with appropriate suitors lead to misunderstandings, poor choices, rejections, growth, maturity, and eventual happiness.

The character of Rev. William Collins offers a morality tale of the short-comings of pastors. Collins and his story gradually shift from silliness to a darker display of pride and presumption in the clerical office.

Collins enters the action as a would-be suitor for one of the Bennet daughters. When he learns that the eldest girl is unavailable, he easily switches his affection to Elizabeth. He sees his proposal as a straightforward business arrangement: as Mr. Bennet's nephew, he will inherit the sonless estate. Elizabeth regards him as a buffoon, and the family views him as overly formal in his manners and a laughable fool.

Collins's early comic role recedes to showcase the pitfalls of conceit and bias. He is flawed in three areas. First, instead of teaching his parishioners to honor God, he is preoccupied with his own advancement and good standing in the eyes of the lady who appointed him to his position as rector in Hunsford. Second, desperately wanting others to be as impressed with his position as he is, he repeatedly mentions the privileges of his post and shows no humility. Third, he is more desirous of advancing his worldly position through marriage than of actually loving and serving a wife.

Collins exhibits none of the biblical marks of a good pastor. Instead, he shows preference for the wealthy, possesses a critical spirit, has no compassion for those who sin, and is self-aggrandizing. In contrast to Collins's disintegrating character, Elizabeth and Darcy move toward humility, acceptance, and happiness. The descent of a pastor is a somber warning against the folly of self-importance and catering to the powerful of this world. Collins is a deftly portrayed character who enters the novel as a merely foolish man and in the end becomes the one example of true arrogance and small-mindedness.

The Private Memoirs and Confessions of a Justified Sinner

Author: James Hogg (1770–1835)

Nationality: Scottish

Date of first publication: 1824

Approximate number of pages: 260

Available editions: numerous editions

Genres: novel, psychological narrative, horror story (gothic fiction), religious fiction, regional writing, melodrama, satire, caricature

Settings for the story: primarily Edinburgh; secondarily a country estate in Scotland in the early eighteenth century in a Presbyterian milieu

Main characters: Robert Wringhim, protagonist; Gil-Martin, Robert's alter ego, or doppelganger, who entices him to a string of misdeeds; George Colwan, Robert's older brother; Rev. Robert Wringhim, adoptive guardian of the protagonist; Laird George Colwan and Lady Dalcastle, parents of Robert and George

Plot summary: A hyper-Calvinistic young man becomes convinced that the elect are justified in ridding the earth of reprobates, so under the influence of a shadowy satanic figure who is actually his alter ego, he goes on a crime spree that includes multiple murders.

Rev. Robert Wringhim is the adoptive father of the protagonist, who is named after him. Although the novel does not overtly say that the protagonist's life in crime is the result of the religious influence of the "reverend father," there is no doubt that the minister's doctrine plays a role. A key event comes when Rev. Wringhim and the protagonist's mother jointly declare him "a justified person," resulting in young Wringhim's assurance of his "freedom from sin" and "the impossibility of [his] falling away from [his] new state." Thus, an issue in ministry raised by the story is the potential for evil that a minister's doctrine and actions can wield on those under his influence.

The story is actually told twice—first by an "editor" who came into possession of a "document," then by the document itself, which is the "private memoirs and confessions" of the protagonist of the story, young Robert Wringhim.

The background to the main action is the ill-advised and improbable marriage of a young heiress from Glasgow to a much older man, Laird George Colwan, owner of a country estate. She is inclined to theological speculation and strict Presbyterianism, and her new husband is a worldling. The marriage produces two sons, the younger of whom is rejected by his biological father and raised by Rev. Robert Wringhim. The heart of the plot is the interaction between the protagonist and his "double," dubbed Gil-Martin, as they together undertake a quest to purge the kirk of reprobates.

❖ ❖ ❖

Saving Grace

Author: Lee Smith (1944–)

Nationality: American

Date of first publication: 1995

Approximate number of pages: 170

Available edition: Ballantine

Genres: novel, local-color writing, Southern fiction, realistic fiction

Setting for the story: the rural Southeast of the United States, specifically North Carolina and Tennessee

Main characters: Florida Grace Shepherd, the protagonist of the story who struggles to move beyond her childhood in a dysfunctional minister's family; Virgil Shepherd, Grace's revivalist father; Mama, Grace's mother who commits suicide over her husband's profligate ways; preacher Travis Wood, whom seventeen-year-old Grace marries when he is forty-two and whom she abandons for another man after bearing two children

Plot summary: This first-person novel traces the life of the protagonist from childhood through midlife. Grace's life is a journey from a childhood tyrannized by her father, through seduction by a half-brother at age fourteen, through marriage at seventeen, through a failed marriage and an adulterous affair with a man named Randy Newhouse. This pilgrimage is of course a journey away from God as Grace perceives him in her father and husband. But the novel moves toward a surprise ending in which Grace returns to the Scrabble Creek of her childhood and embraces the religion in which she had been raised.

One of the master strokes of this novel is its ambiguous title. At the level of plot, the title names the central action of the story—saving Grace Shepherd (with the family name itself possessing symbolic overtones) from a life of sin and failure. But at a thematic level, the story is about God's saving grace as it contends with wayward humanity (chiefly those who profess Christianity).

The religious world of the novel moves between the two poles of revivalist fundamentalism and ascetic holiness, as represented by the two ministers in

Grace's life. One is her snake-handling, adulterous father who spreads the gospel through his personal charisma. The other is her life-denying husband. Although the protagonist of the story rejects the God projected by her father and husband, she does not disbelieve in the existence of God, despite her running from him.

The novel brings numerous issues in ministry to light. A brief list includes the following: perplexity over how we should understand the "signs and wonders" of religion, the positive effects and perils of a charismatic minister, extremism in devotion to ministry, sexual temptation in a minister's life, the effect of success on a minister, and unworthy ministers as an obstacle to the gospel.

◆—◆—◆

Scenes of Clerical Life

Author: George Eliot (pen name of Mary Ann Evans) (1819–80)

Nationality: English

Date of first publication: 1858

Approximate number of pages: 610

Available editions: numerous editions

Genres: novella, historical fiction

Setting for the story: Shepperton, England

Main characters: Rev. Amos Barton and Milly Barton; Mr. Gilfil and Tina; Janet Dempster and Rev. Tryan

Plot summary: This book is a series of three novellas that look at aspects of human love through the lens of three clergymen.

The Sad Fortunes of the Reverend Amos Barton" is a depiction of an average human who is struck by deep tragedy. Amos is a somewhat pretentious vicar. His sense of himself and his intellect are overblown, and the majority of his parishioners are bemused at his own self-valuation. Eliot describes Amos as the fortunate recipient of love from a soul far better than himself, namely, his wife, Milly. Amos's life is changed when Milly dies. Unable to attract love from any other, he becomes lovable through the death of the only one who truly loved him. Milly's passing opens up the hearts of his parishioners, who become devoted to their vicar.

"Mr. Gilfil's Love Story" explores the theme of the soul that has loved and lost and is thereafter unable to love again. Gilfil is described as a stolid and serene fellow, a man who seems cold and uncaring. It is a surprise, then, to learn that in his youth Gilfil had loved with passion. The object of his love was Tina, who in turn was loved and disappointed by another. After much tragedy, the two ended up together, but his bliss was cut short by Tina's death. Gilfil's heart was closed forever. He was a man who could love passionately but could never love again.

"Janet's Repentance" revolves around the relationship between Janet Demp- ster and Rev. Tryan. Janet is a once-beautiful and vivacious woman who became trapped in a difficult marriage to a drunkard. Tryan was a dissenter in the Church of England who challenged the established ways of the church and sought to bring the gospel back to the people of England. The relationship between Tryan and Janet is a relationship of mutual affection and reliance in which two people guide each other through illness and loss.

In each of these stories, Eliot depicts the souls of the clergy. She takes us into the hearts of these three men, revealing there the same tumultuous inner life that afflicts all humanity. Eliot humanizes the clergy, uncovering the forces of love, loss, and grief that are revealed through her penetrating gaze.

⊰◆◆◆⊱

A Simple Honorable Man

Author: Conrad Richter (1890–1968)

Nationality: American

Date of first publication: 1962

Approximate number of pages: 310

Available edition: Knopf

Genre: novel

Setting for the story: several small towns in rural Pennsylvania

Main character: Harry Donner, a Lutheran pastor

Plot summary: Almost forty, Harry Donner, a small-town store owner who never graduated from high school, decides to pursue a career in the ministry. He relocates his wife and children to Port Oxford, where he can begin his preparation at West Shore College and Seminary. Donner spends several pleasant years studying and preaching "on supply." After graduating, he receives his first call to a rural parish, where he feels particularly drawn to the nearby poverty-stricken mining com- munities, especially Lost Cove, which causes murmuring among his parishioners. He establishes a small church in Lost Cove before moving to his next parish in a lovely locale but with a congregation with serious problems. After dealing for several years with this congregation's inner and outer turmoil, Donner is briefly tempted by an offer from a large congregation in Brooklyn. He eventually settles in a drab mining town. In the neighboring mountain settlements, Donner makes inroads with the unchurched, bringing them Word and sacrament and fulfilling his own true sense of mission. Several years later, after his wife's death, he is still ministering to the elderly in the Eureka Hotel, where he lives, and in the neighboring mining communities. When Donner passes away, he leaves behind no money but the legacy of two churches he built and three sons who understand his calling imperfectly.

This novel has at its core the Lutheran understanding of vocation, which places God's call at the core of being. Harry Donner does not agonize over his choices; he simply responds to the opportunities God places in front of him. Donner's call is a gift from God, as free as grace. It is not a duty or a sacrifice; neither does it involve a conscious effort to reflect the glory of God in his work. It is instead a response to the forgiveness of sins, which Donner in turn continually offers to his parishioners, some of whom are unlovely and unloved.

The title of this book says it all: this is a redemptive story of a virtuous, simple, honorable man—a positive picture of a pastor uncommon in modern literature. The incidents Donner confronts contain their own drama (murder, suicide, abuse, destruction), but the overwhelming effect of this book is to make the reader see how much there is to admire and emulate in what appears to be a quiet life, unremarkably lived if measured by worldly standards. It is about Harry Donner as God's instrument in pouring the extravagance of grace upon a world that does not seem to deserve it.

Starbridge Series

Author: Susan Howatch (1940–)

Nationality: English

Date of first publication: *Glittering Images*, 1987; *Glamorous Powers*, 1988; *Ultimate Prizes*, 1989; *Scandalous Risks*, 1990; *Mystical Paths*, 1992; *Absolute Truths*, 1995

Approximate number of pages: between 400 and 600 (each)

Available edition: Fawcett

Genres: novel, historical fiction, regional writing, family saga

Setting for the story: the fictional Anglican diocese of Starbridge and its cathedral

Main characters: Rev. Charles Ashworth, a Cambridge academic sent to investigate possible sexual scandals at Starbridge; Jonathan Darrow, a Fordite monk and spiritual healer; Neville Aysgarth, who begins as a young, ambitious archdeacon of Starbridge and becomes dean of Starbridge Cathedral; Venetia Flaxton, who has an affair with Aysgarth

Plot summary: Although the novels can stand alone, they should be read chronologically to get the full effect. The action in the series centers on Starbridge Cathedral, and the overall story lifts the curtain on the inner workings of the Church of England from the late 1930s through the 1960s. The novels show the main characters grappling with the social issues confronting the Church of England during the time frame covered in the story. In some ways the fictitious Starbridge Cathedral is another character, having a hold on the cast of human characters who are drawn to it.

The series begins and ends with Charles Ashworth. In the first book, *Glittering Images*, Charles is sent as a junior member in the church's hierarchy to investigate Bishop Adam Alexander Jardine and a "potentially disastrous indiscretion." Once there, Charles faces an intense moral and spiritual crisis that shakes his faith. His spiritual mentor is Father Jonathan Darrow, a charismatic healer and complicated human, who is the narrator of the second book, *Glamorous Powers*. The story is continued in the third book, *Ultimate Prizes*, which focuses on power-hungry Neville Aysgarth.

Scandalous Risks and *Mystical Paths* introduce the next generation of laity and leadership in the Church of England, with Venetia Flaxton and Nicholas Darrow, Jonathan Darrow's son, ensconced at St. Benet's Rectory and its healing center. Nicholas, like his father, has the gift of healing. In the final novel, *Absolute Truths*, the series comes full circle and returns to Charles Ashworth.

Issues in ministry portrayed in the series include the following: church authority and hierarchy; sexual misconduct and immorality among church leaders; clerical ambition and power; the role of healing, visions, and miracles in ministry; the church's response to a rapidly changing culture; and crisis of faith in church leaders.

The Sunday Wife

Author: Cassandra King (1944–)

Nationality: American

Date of first publication: 2002

Approximate number of pages: 560

Available edition: Hyperion

Genres: novel, domestic fiction

Setting for the story: Crystal Springs, a Florida Panhandle town

Main characters: Dean Lynch, wife of the new Methodist minister; Augusta Holderfield, the impetuous woman who befriends Dean

Plot summary: The novel looks at the inward reflection of Dean Lynch and her desire to change her circumstances. Uncomfortable in her role as a minister's wife, Dean feels she can only do what is expected and not what she truly desires. Through Augusta, Dean is introduced to a new perspective. As a result, she questions her role in her husband's ministry and ultimately pits herself against her husband on various issues.

As a minister's wife, Dean wants to help her husband, Ben, succeed in his ministry, but she resents living in the rectory instead of having a home of her own. She is happy to take part in church activities, but too frequently she is the subject of the church ladies' gossip. Her own faith feels stifled by the act she puts on to be the proper Sunday wife. Her husband has ambitions to advance in the denomination, and she knows he expects her to subsume her own desires in order to promote his career. Because of her backwoods upbringing and her personality, she is often unsure whether she is a help or a hindrance, and her husband is adept at pointing out her flaws.

While Dean might have felt uneasy enough on her own, her friendship with Augusta Holderfield pushes her into new territory, leading Dean to question her role as ministry helpmate, as the one who comes behind and covers over Ben's weaknesses, taking blame for things that are not her doing and receiving little credit for things that are her successes. Ben resents Augusta's influence, but he is unsuccessful in blocking her from Dean's life. As Augusta brings Dean into a circle of friends that includes the local fortune-teller and a homosexual couple wanting to marry in Ben's church, Dean repeatedly has to choose whether she will side with Ben and his congregation or the people who have brought her light and joy. Ultimately, Augusta's secrets force Dean to deal with her friend's selfishness and to examine what seems to be her own increasingly empty life.

Dean's life illustrates the challenges faced by some ministers' wives. She sees her husband's growing self-absorption and neglectfulness. She is an outcast among the church members because she fails to conform to their ideas of what a minister's wife should be and do. She feels hemmed in, ill-fitted, unappreciated, and unfairly judged. As ties loosen and an opportunity to have a different life arises, Dean tries to determine who she is and what makes her happy.

The Testament of Gideon Mack

Author: James Robertson (1958–)

Nationality: Scottish

Date of first publication: 2006

Approximate number of pages: 400

Available editions: Penguin, Viking

Genres: novel, regional or local-color writing, psychological fiction

Setting for the story: Monimasket, a small Scottish seaside town

Main characters: Gideon Mack, a Church of Scotland minister; the devil

Plot summary: Working as a minister despite his atheism is uncomfortable at times for Gideon Mack, but on the whole he is content with doing good deeds and tending to his community. When he reappears three days after being pre-sumed dead following a plunge into a local river gorge, he tells a wild tale of being rescued by the devil. Though he still doesn't believe God is at work in the world, he now knows the devil is. When Gideon insists on telling this story to the world, both verbally and in the manuscript that makes up this book, many question whether Gideon is telling the truth, has gone mad, or is a liar.

Gideon Mack becomes famous when he emerges after three days, rela-tively unscathed, from a tumultuous waterway known locally as the "Black Jaws." Though it seems he was rescued by a fisherman, Mack begins to understand that a local legend is true: the devil keeps his home in a cave at the bottom of the falls. Mack was rescued by the devil and brought back to health in that very cave before being sent back to the world.

Since Mack is both a self-professed atheist and a practicing Church of Scotland minister, his newfound belief in the existence of the devil (but not God) causes an uproar in his seaside Scottish town and beyond.

While people are intrigued by his story, most do not believe him, thinking him either mad or, more charitably, damaged by his experience in the water.

In a final attempt to help people understand his story, Mack writes a memoir, beginning with his melancholy childhood and tracing the events that led him to be an unbelieving minister, a distant husband, an unfaithful friend, and ultimately a man desirous of the devil's company.

Sandwiched between a prologue and an epilogue written by an editor who was given Gideon Mack's strange tale is Mack's own account of the paths that brought him to belief in the supernatural, a view of the character and work of the devil unapproved by the presbytery. Mack leaves this manuscript and goes off in search of the devil. No one sees him alive again. The question for the editor, and for the reader, is whether Mack is a trustworthy narrator. If so, the continuing existence of God is in doubt, and the devil is weary of his work disrupting the world.

The Thanatos Syndrome

Author: Walker Percy (1916–90)

Nationality: American

Date of first publication: 1987

Approximate number of pages: 370

Available editions: Picador, Ballantine, Ivy

Genres: novel, thriller, local-color writing, medical fiction

Settings for the story: southern United States, mainly Feliciana Parish, Louisiana; short, remembered scenes from Nazi Germany

Main characters: Thomas More, protagonist, named for martyred sixteenth-century author of *Utopia*, a psychiatrist recently imprisoned on drug charges and facing down entrenched power that seeks pleasure and social control; More is helped by his bright, attractive cousin Lucy Lipscomb and a failed alcoholic priest, Simon Smith, who runs a hospice and shelter for society's rejects

Plot summary: Thomas More follows clues from psychiatric patients, family, and others to heroically expose a social engineering project called "Blue Boy," which laces the water supply with heavy sodium from the nuclear generating plant. The result is ape-like behavior accompanied by sharp declines in crime and various diseases and sharp increases in math skills and factual recall. More is aided technically by epidemiologist Lucy Lipscomb (after a brief affair, both return to their spouses). With More's intervention, the ironically named Qualitarian Center, where the unwanted are euthanized and quality of life replaces divinity of life, is transformed into Smith's life-affirming hospice, staffed by various broken characters now given new purpose.

Walker Percy's final novel evaluates modern human dysfunction. Readers of C. S. Lewis's *Abolition of Man* (prose) and *That Hideous Strength* (fiction) will recognize important thematic parallels: reason unguided by morality sacrifices free moral choice in exchange for a socially engineered utopia. The title's *Thanatos* (Greek god of death) suggests a culture of death. Echoing Flannery O'Connor (*Mystery and Manners*), the character Simon Smith observes that "tenderness"—abstract love for humanity or the social good without morality—leads "to the gas chambers!" The devil simply left us alone, and we did the rest: "Reason warred with faith. Science triumphed. . . . One hundred million dead."

The priest in the novel, Father Smith, though unconventional and "failed," fulfills the essential pastoral roles of reproving the errant, delivering a prophetic word, and caring for the sick and needy, as do other "failed" characters who follow his model and direction. Ministry issues abound, presented unconventionally through flawed characters. They include the following: failed priests/ministers, denominational extremes, eugenics, euthanasia, abortion, alcoholism, psychiatric pathology, sexual obsession (often explicit), race, environmentalism, and the individual versus society.

Thomas Wingfold, Curate

Author: George MacDonald (1824–1905)

Nationality: Scottish

Date of first publication: 1876

Approximate number of pages: 500

Available editions: multiple; this novel was and is still sometimes published as three volumes, even though it is one story

Genres: novel, religious fiction, murder story, small-town fiction

Setting for the story: a small fictional town called Glaston in England in the Victorian era

Main characters: Thomas Wingfold, protagonist, twenty-six-year-old curate of the local Anglican church; Helen Lingard, twenty-three-year-old unmarried parishioner and focal point of many of the relationships in the novel; Helen's beloved brother Leopold, a student at Cambridge University who commits a murder and hides out in Glaston; Joseph Polwarth, a misshapen dwarf who becomes Wingfold's chief spiritual advisor; George Bascombe, cynical cousin and suitor of Helen Lingard

Plot summary: The story begins with a picture of small-town, Church of England, nominal Christianity in which people attend church but are not true Christians. The inciting moment in this spectacle of spiritual deadness comes when young George Bascombe has the nerve to ask Curate Wingfold how much of the Christian faith he actually believes. The curate concludes that he is not even a true believer. The main plotline of the story is Wingfold's journey into faith and the impact this has on the spiritual development of other characters in the novel.

Thomas Wingfold begins his pastoral career as an unbeliever, viewing the church as no more than a religious and social institution. The bombshell that sets ripples in motion is dropped by a cynical young man from London, George Bascombe, who as he accompanies the curate home after a dinner party points to the church building and asks Wingfold if he believes "one word of all that." Upon later reflection, Wingfold concludes that he is totally without personal conviction regarding the Christian faith.

Two main plotlines flow outward from this moment of crisis in the life of the local curate. One is the story of Wingfold's coming to faith and the changes this instigates in his personal life and in the discharge of his pastoral duties, including preaching. The second, accompanying story is about the spiritual growth that Wingfold's ministry now initiates in the lives of others, especially those in crisis.

Issues in ministry are multiple: the hypocrisy of a minister not believing what he preaches, the need for a minister to be a true convert, the riskiness of plagiarizing sermons, the key role that parishioners with spiritual discernment can play in a minister's life and ministry, and the glory and efficacy of a minister's vocation when he is a true shepherd of his flock.

The Vicar of Wakefield

Author: Oliver Goldsmith (1728–74)

Nationality: Irish

Date of first publication: 1766

Approximate number of pages: 175

Available editions: numerous editions

Genres: novel, satire

Setting for the story: eighteenth-century English countryside

Main characters: Dr. Primrose, the vicar; the wicked squire Thornhill; Mr. Burchell

Plot summary: Beset by a series of Job-like misfortunes (mostly the result of his and his family's naiveté and vanity), the vicar nevertheless maintains his principles, his trust in providence, and his generous spirit.

The joy of Dr. Primrose, the vicar of Wakefield, is his family of six children. He is a man of principles, for which he is willing to face all manner of trials. His oldest son's wedding to his true love is canceled. His wealth is lost by a dishonest steward. His oldest daughter is dishonored by a deceiving squire. Finally, Dr. Primrose lands in prison after incurring the wrath of that same squire. Salvation comes through an unsuspecting character, and the story concludes with a happy ending.

The novel is neither a moral tale about the triumph of moral principles nor a sentimental story about tragedy ending happily. Rather, Oliver Goldsmith presents a light satire that invites us to enjoy a quick-paced tale of misadventures by which he pokes fun at the pretenses of social and literary conventions of the day. The undoing of the vicar is due as much to his own foibles as to the ill intentions of the wicked. Dr. Primrose stands rigidly on both great and small principles. He is naive about the intentions of those who are deceitful, and that naiveté is exploited by appeals to his vanity, as well as his family's.

And yet the vicar's virtues keep the reader humorously sympathetic. He has a good heart. He is generous, hospitable, sincere, and forgiving. One cannot feel too troubled by his misfortunes, because the minister himself refuses to be so. Most of all, he loves his family members, who though generally foolish are truly happy together.

The book exalts virtue and religion, but there is a lack of gospel elements. The vicar speaks of providence and heaven, for which we strive through our moral efforts, making the best of whatever befalls us. There is no mention of Christ, and sinners are beseeched to reform themselves. The vicar has a noble heart, to be sure, but evidently one that he obtained with the help of providence.

Wheat That Springeth Green

Author: J. F. Powers (1917–99)

Nationality: American

Date of first publication: 1988

Approximate number of pages: 335

Available edition: Alfred A. Knopf

Genre: semiautobiographical novel (*Bildungsroman*)

Setting for the story: a Midwestern American town in the mid-twentieth century

Main characters: Joe Hackett, protagonist and priest; Father Van Slaag; Father William Stock; Father Felix

Plot summary: The novel follows the life of Joe Hackett as he grows up from a little boy to a high school track star and then to a forty-four-year-old priest. Disenchanted with the clerical life, he goes through the motions in his ministry to his middle-class parish without joy or devotion. But when his new assistant Bill arrives straight out of seminary, Joe is inspired to step up his act and mentor him.

Jennifer Powers wrote in the introduction to this, her father's novel, "Written over an increasingly dark time, *Wheat That Springeth Green* was shaped by my father's growing conviction of the progressive and irredeemable absurdity of things. He was a connoisseur of the dull, the mediocre, and the second-rate, and of the disingenuous and fraudulent, but now it seemed that their dominion has truly come." Powers crafted a fingerprint for the modern midlevel clergy in *Wheat That Springeth Green*.

Joe Hackett had aspired to be a saintly man of the church since his early childhood, but the toils of seminary life and later of apprenticeship dampened his enthusiasm for the trade. His rise in the church was paralleled by a fall in his personal interest and passion for the life of a cleric, and as he eventually headed his own church, he traded a devotional life for modern comforts and worldly habits.

Hackett struggles to maintain his religious leadership, balancing the demands for financial stability of the church through an increase in collections with the need to support local business and weigh in on ethical decisions, all with a backdrop of the Vietnam War. He is a disinterested priest who desires to avoid having to deal with problems but cannot do so and who despite himself chooses to do the right thing.

This book is a true portrait of modern American life for the cleric. It is a frank account of an ordinary man who aspires to live for God and the honest tale of how he is made and remade as a priest. Powers creates an archetype of the lukewarm clergyman to whom believers can relate, hoping for a revival in their faith. Readers come to know Hackett not just as a priest but also as he was before he was ordained, evoking compassion as we share his struggles, tribulations, and triumphs in believing again.

Wise Blood

Author: Flannery O'Connor (1925–64)

Nationality: American

Date of first publication: 1952

Approximate number of pages: 230

Available edition: Farrar, Straus and Giroux

Genres: novel, comedy, Southern gothic with grotesque and comedic elements

Setting for the story: Taulkinham, a fictional Southern town in the post–World War II era

Main characters: Hazel (Haze) Motes, a soldier turned street preacher; Enoch Emery, a guard at the town zoo who has "wise blood"; Asa Hawks, a phony blind street preacher; Sabbath Lily, Hawks's teenaged daughter; Slade, a used-car salesman; Hoover Shoats and Solace Layfield, two shady preachers; Mrs. Flood, Motes's nosy landlady

Plot summary: *Wise Blood* depicts the anguished tensions in the soul and life of a would-be street preacher named Hazel Motes. In his supposed quest to rid himself of both the true Jesus and his atonement, Motes encounters a gallery of characters in a small Southern city. Each of them parries with him as a foil or a friend, but they all spiral downward into fraud, debauchery, and blindness. Motes's quest ends not with a new "Church Without Christ," as he envisions, but with his own blindness and death instead.

Hazel Motes, just out of the army after World War II, sets out by train from his now-abandoned home in Eastrod, Tennessee, for the town of Taulkinham. Disillusioned with his traditional faith, Motes fancies himself a preacher of a different sort—one who doesn't believe in Jesus. On his first night in the town, he tells a prostitute as much and states that he plans to start a new church, "The Church Without Christ."

The scattered plot then weaves its way around Motes's interplay with an assortment of eccentric characters. *Wise Blood* parades these curious people around Motes and his quest for meaning. He is suspicious of Asa Hawks, a supposedly blind street preacher. Enoch Emery, a young guard at the zoo, follows Motes around and tries to convince him that he has found in a shrunken mummy the "new jesus." Because Emery thinks he possesses insights into life's mysteries, or "wise blood," as he calls it, he tries to convince Motes that this mysterious artifact holds the secret to truth. Motes's fortunes begin to plummet when a rival preacher, Onnie Jay Holy (real name Hoover Shoats), touts his own prophet, Solace Layfield, as Motes's rival. Motes runs over Layfield with his car and kills him. After vain attempts at self-flagellation to atone, he wanders off and is subsequently found dead.

Wise Blood engages ministry issues such as personal integrity in clerical life; the nature of the gospel's redemptive message, both truly and falsely held; how to express true faith in modern times; and the danger of twisting the Bible's meaning to advance personal or ecclesiological goals.

Woman of the Pharisees

Author: François Mauriac (1885–1970)

Nationality: French

Date of first publication: 1941

Approximate number of pages: 240

Available edition: Avalon Publishing Group

Genres: novel, regional or local-color writing

Settings for the story: the French countryside in the early 1900s prior to World War I, primarily the small town of Baluzac and the nearby country estate of Larjuzon

Main characters: Abbé Calou, curé of Baluzac; Brigitte Pian, mistress of Larjuzon and benefactress of Calou; Louis Pian, Brigitte's stepson and narrator of the book; Jean de Mirbel, Louis's school friend sent to live with Calou; Michelé, Louis's sister

Plot summary: The story is narrated retrospectively by Brigitte Pian's stepson, Louis, who draws from his childhood memories as well as diaries and letters to describe significant events in the lives of his family, friends, and Abbé Calou.

Abbé Calou is an aged priest who acts as curé to the humble parish of Baluzac in the French countryside. He is a loving and gentle man who spends most of his time studying and praying, with occasional visits to check on his flock. Despite feeling that he is of little use to most of his parishioners, he continues to devote great care to his sermons in the hope that they will reach any seeking souls who come through the church doors. The priest's parish is only a few miles from the country estate of Larjuzon, home to Brigitte Pian, her husband, and her two stepchildren. Brigitte Pian is benefactress of Calou. She is a cold and self-righteous woman with strict religious principles. As a result, she continually interferes in the lives of all those around her in an effort to better their souls and save them from damnation.

The main action in the novel is the parallel transformation that Calou and Brigitte undergo in their understanding of Christian love. The instigation for this transformation is the arrival of Jean de Mirbel, a troublesome boy sent to live with Calou. Soon after he arrives, Jean and Brigitte's stepdaughter fall in love and begin seeing each other secretly.

The adults' subsequent interference leads to disaster, and it is through this that Calou and Brigitte gain insight into their own character flaws. Calou observes that though they erred in opposite directions, the root of their error was the same. They took it upon themselves to save the souls of others in the name of Christian love. Once they learn that changing destinies is a task reserved for God alone, both Calou and Brigitte are finally able to experience and participate in the ministry of true Christian love.

Young Goodman Brown

Author: Nathaniel Hawthorne (1804–64)

Nationality: American

Date of first publication: 1835 in magazine form; 1846 in *Mosses from an Old Manse*

Approximate number of pages: 15

Available editions: various anthologies of American literature; editions of Hawthorne's major works

Genres: short story, fantasy, gothic fiction, allegory or symbolism

Setting for the story: Salem, Massachusetts, and the adjoining forest, at the end of the seventeenth century

Main characters: Young Goodman Brown, a typical young man in the Puritan milieu of the story (his name is the Puritan equivalent of "Everyman"); the most visible and revered leaders of the community (such as minister and deacon)

Plot summary: Young Goodman Brown begins the story determined to make a nighttime journey into the forest to transact an unspecified matter. Parting from his wife, Faith, he undertakes his perilous journey. The farther he journeys into the forest, the more it takes on supernatural and demonic attributes. Equally unsettling is the fact that the citizens who are the most revered public exemplars of virtue are all in the evil forest. The climax of the forest event is a demonic ritual that binds all the attendees together in a brotherhood of evil. Young Goodman Brown returns to the village the next morning to live as a morbid recluse.

This story has been interpreted in so many contradictory ways that the commentary has gone a long way toward ruining the story. This is inexcusable, inasmuch as Nathaniel Hawthorne has inserted his meaning explicitly into the story. The experience portrayed in the story is a naive young man's discovery that everyone—including public icons of goodness and he himself—possesses an evil heart that is ordinarily hidden from public view.

The external sign or symbol of this universal evil is the dark forest. The "faith" that Young Goodman Brown loses is his faith in the goodness of people. A dark master of ceremonies at the demonic ritual tells the "converts" at the service, "There [pointing to the people in the forest] are all whom ye have reverenced from youth. Ye deemed them holier than yourselves. . . . Now ye are undeceived."

The story asserts what we all know to be true, namely, that all people, including publicly acclaimed figures of goodness, have a dual nature: they are evil (hence their presence in the forest) and good (as they live in daylight in the village). As readers we are asked to acknowledge this fact and determine how to negotiate it. Young Goodman Brown chooses the path of total disillusionment, becoming "a distrustful, if not a desperate man." Hawthorne does not offer his choice as a necessary one. We must all ask, however, what is the right way to live with a knowledge of hidden sin in other people, including religious leaders?

184

Leland Ryken has taught English at Wheaton College since 1968. He has had a speaking and writing career in addition to a teaching career. He has published over three dozen books on a range of topics, including the Bible as literature, literature and the arts in Christian perspective, work and leisure, the Puritans, guides to the literary classics, the Christian imagination, the English Bible translation, and the legacy of the King James Bible. His areas of expertise in literature include Milton, Shakespeare, seventeenth-century English literature, and the Bible as literature.

Philip Ryken is the eighth president of Wheaton College, where he studied literature with his father, Leland, and graduated with a degree in English and philosophy. After studying pastoral ministry at Westminster Theological Seminary and earning a doctorate in historical theology from the University of Oxford, he preached for fifteen years at the historic Tenth Presbyterian Church in Philadelphia. He is the author of more than thirty expository commentaries, reference tools, and other books for the church on ministry, discipleship, Christianity, and culture.

Todd Wilson is the senior pastor of Calvary Memorial Church in Oak Park, Illinois. Previously he served on the pastoral staff at College Church in Wheaton, Illinois, and Bethlehem Baptist Church in Minneapolis, Minnesota. Todd graduated from Wheaton College with a BA in philosophy and an MA in biblical exegesis. He completed a PhD in New Testament at Cambridge University and is the author of several articles and books, including *Preach the Word: Essays on Expository Preaching: In Honor of R. Kent Hughes*, edited with Leland Ryken. Todd and his wife, Katie, have five children—three biological and two twin boys they adopted from Ethiopia.

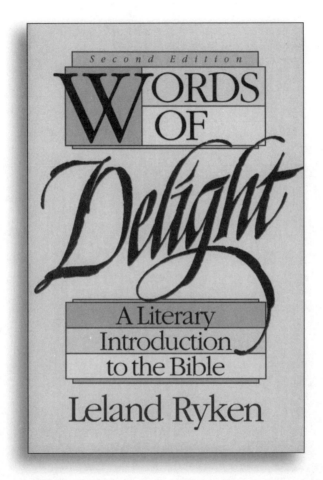

Also by
LELAND RYKEN

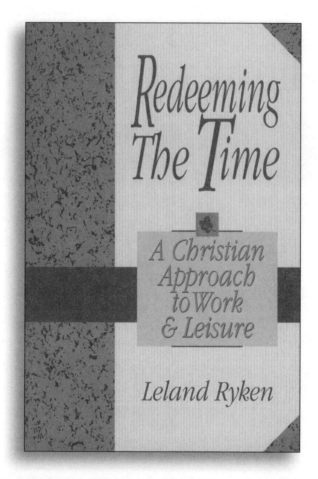

This fully developed biblical perspective of work and leisure finds the enjoyment of both as a holistic balance often missing today.

TEACH STUDENTS HOW TO TEACH THE BIBLE BETTER

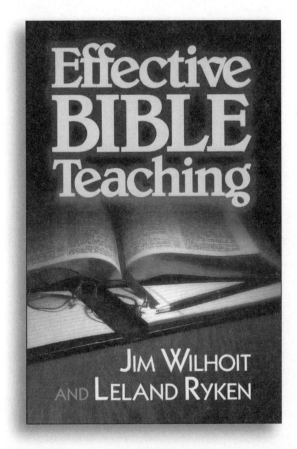

In a readable and practical style, these specialists in Christian education provide students with the knowledge and methods needed to effectively communicate the message of the Bible to others.